Be Good To Yourself
- Edited by Ross Books

Library of Congress Cataloging-in-Publication Data
Marden, Orison Swett, 1848-1924.
Be good to yourself / by Orison Swett Marden ;
edited by Ross Books.   p. cm.
ISBN 978-0-89496-005-5 (pbk) --
ISBN 978-0-89496-006-2 (hbk)
ISBN 978-0-89496-007-9 (ebook)
1. Conduct of life. I. Title.
BJ1581.M2 2010
158--dc22
2009039981

Orison Sewett Marden (1850-1924)

Ross Books
P.O. Box 4340
Berkeley, Ca.94704
Copyright © 2010 Ross Books
www.rossbooks.com

BE GOOD TO YOURSELF

- Edited by Ross Books

By Orison Swett Marden

Preface

Orison Swett Marden is considered to be the founder of the modern success movement in America. It is hard to deny this because Marden's first book, *Pushing to the Front*, was published in 1894 and had a phenomenal circulation. Then in 1897 he founded *Success Magazine*, which reached the enormous circulation, for that time, of nearly a half-million. This means, of course, that it was read by from two to three million readers. Through his magazine and his many books he honed the skill of actualizing success to perfection. Although his ideas are as needed and true today as a hundred years ago, the writing is hopelessly out of date because of the great difference in culture.

In an effort to bring his thoughts back to life in today's world we decided to edit and rewrite one of his most famous works *Be Good To Yourself*. Examples like the coal burning fire engine are replaced with modern analogies, things like eBooks are introduced and sexism is removed from the language. Otherwise we remained true to his original work and we only made changes where necessary.

We chose *Be Good To Yourself* because this title was written right at the height of his career and it is targeted at the successful business person. The book defines the traits which prevent success and explores the thinking habits that often create our failures.

In a positive but forceful manner the author explains how to escape or avoid the traps that so often cripple our careers and our businesses. One of the great gifts of Marden's style of speech and analysis is that he avoids the jargon and psychological language that is so often found in success books.

Table of Contents

I have wished a bird would fly away,
And not sing by my house all day;

Have clapped my hands at him from the door
When it seemed as if I could bear no more.

The fault must partly have been in me.
The bird was not to blame for his key.

And of course there must be something wrong
In wanting to silence any song.

Robert Frost

Chapter 1

Be Good To Yourself

It is great to meet a person who has a wonderful personality and is completely in control of all their undertakings – a person who approachs their everyday tasks with the assurance of a winner. Such a person is able to deal vigrously with all their life's problems. They keep themselves in condition to do their best and do the most difficult thing easily. You can watch them seize in a masterly fashion the precious opportunities which come their way.

In order to obtain complete mastery of all their powers and possibilities they must be good to themselves. They must be able to think well of themselves and protect themselves in whatever situations they are placed.

A friend of mine once said that anyone who belittles their self and their possibilities does injustice to the nature of the universe. Very few people, he said, think well enough of them-selves or respect their abilities, their character and their dor-mant abilities.

People who persist in accenting the weak, the diseased, and the erring side of themselves do so for various reasons. They may believe that they have inherited bad traits or been poorly brought up. They may think that they are educationally de-prived—that they never had a chance. Others think, simply, that they do not amount to much and never will. They are *always* exaggerating their defects. Because they see only the pettiness of their lives they never grow into well-developed adults. They have barren self-images which do little to help them construct their lives. Their appearance and their ambitions express their poor opinions of themselves. They actually think themselves into weak and ineffective careers.

As a person thinks in their heart, so are they.

One's opinion of oneself is expressed outwardly. If you want to make the most of yourself never picture yourself as anything different from the man or woman that you long to become. Whenever you think of yourself form a mental image of a being who possesses every desirable quality. Refuse to see anything about yourself which would detract from your per-sonality. Insist upon seeing only this positive image of the man or woman nature intended and not the distorted man or woman which your ignorance or unfortunate environment have pro-duced. The image of yourself that you carry in your mind, your self-esteem, will mean infinitely more to you than what other people may think. You will grow to fulfill your positive self-image. In order to make the most of our lives we must not only think well of ourselves we must be good to our bodies.

It is just as necessary to cultivate the health, strength and beauty of the body as it is to cultivate the vigor of the mind.

There are plenty of people who are good to others but are not good to themselves. They do not take care of their health or conserve their energies and resources. They are slaves to others and tyrants to themselves.

Faithfulness to others is an attractive trait yet faithfulness to yourself is equally important. You owe it to yourself to take care of your health and this means both physical and mental health. It is everyone's duty to keep them self in condition to answer any demands that an emergency might make upon them. There are many able people whose careers are disappointing bad simply because they do not keep themselves in the best physical and mental condition. In every place of business we find employees who are only half awake, half alive; their bodies are the victims of bad habits in living and in thinking. Is it any wonder that they get so little out of life when they put so little into it?

I know middle-aged people who are, as far as their accomplishments in life go, just where they were when they left high school or college. They have not advanced a bit. Some have even regressed. They cannot understand why they are not more successful. But everyone who knows them sees their great handicaps— indifference to their health, neglect of their physical needs, wasted energy, bad living habits, etc. Everywhere we see young men and women plodding along in their careers, capable of great things, but doing little, because they are not vigorous in overcoming the obstacles in their paths. They have not been good to their physical selves.

I am sure you have experienced reading an author's book that is lifeless. It does not capture the reader's attention because it lacks vitality. It does not arouse a positive response because the author was not enthusiastic when they wrote it. Another example is a priest that does not reach their people because they lack stamina, force and physical vitality or a teacher that does not arouse their pupils' interest in a subject, or inspire them to excel because the teacher them self lacks enthusiasm. Their brain and nerves are weary, their energy exhausted, their strength depleted, because they have not been good to them selves.

Everywhere we see devitalized people, without spontaneity, buoyancy, or enthusiasm in their endeavour. They have no joy in their work. For them, their tasks are merely enforced drudgery, shaping their lives in a dreary monotonous routine.

The great goal in industry is to obtain the greatest possible results with the least possible expenditure of money and the least wear and tear on machinery. Therefore, many people study the economics of getting the maximum return from minimum expenditures yet few of these people who are so shrewd and level-headed in their business pay attention to the economy of their own personal power.

Most of us are at war with ourselves, we are our own worst enemies. We expect a great deal of ourselves, yet we do not put ourselves in condition to achieve great things. We are too self-indulgent or we do not sufficiently indulge good things for our bodies which are the machines that are supposed to produce so much energy and action. Whenever we pamper or neglect ourselves, it is difficult to tell which mode of treatment produces worse results. Few people treat their bodies with the same wise care and consideration that they bestow upon valuable machinery or property of any kind.

The digestive apparatus, for example, which can be thought of as supplying motor power for the whole body is often given only half a chance to do its work properly. The digestive organs of many people are exhausted in trying to assimilate surplus or improper food. This hampers the necessary digestive processes.

People are constantly violating the laws of health. They eat all sorts of indigestible food and often when the stomach is exhausted and unable to take even a bland diet. After stuffing themselves they retard the digestive processes with harmful drinks. Then they wonder why they are unfit for work and resort to all sorts of stimulants and drugs to overcome the bad effects of their thoughtless self-indulgence.

Many go to the other extreme and do not eat enough food or have a sufficiently varied diet so that some of their tissues are in a chronic condition of semi-starvation. The result is a nutritional imbalance which tends to induce an abnormal appetite for food and alcohol. Many people resort to dangerous drugs in their effort to satisfy the craving of their starved tissues when what they really need is nourishing food.

If only most of us would study the needs of our bodies as we study the needs of the plants in our gardens and give them the proper amount of food, with plenty of water, fresh air, and sunshine we would not be troubled with disorders of the stomach, headaches or most other aches or pains. For most of us common sense in our diet would do away with the need for frequent medication. A bad diet can cripple our lives and our careers. Economize in other things if you must, wear threadbare clothes if necessary, but never cheat your body or brain in the quality and quantity of your food.

The most precious investment a person can make is in their health.

Ambitious farmers select the finest ears of corn and the finest grain, fruits and vegetables for seed. They cannot afford to plant their soil with bad seed. Can the person who is ambitious to make the most of them self afford to eat cheap stale food which has lost its appeal and nutritional value?

Everywhere we see business people eating indigestible food and snacking on junk food, drinking artificial beverages, and using too many stimulants. Long ago I used to travel by train with a businessman who was financially better off than me but who would never take a sleeper at night or go into a dining car for his meals. Instead he would live on sandwiches or whatever he could pick up at lunch-counters on the route. The result was that when he arrived at his destination he would be so tired and his stomach so out of order from irregular eating that it would take him several days to get straightened out. He lost a good deal of valuable time in this fashion

Nowadays the most extensive travel is by air. The airlines cater to fat expense accounts and serve food and beverages to their customers and provide for their comfort in many ways. Yet many people in business are still disoriented by travel. They are unfamiliar with the area they are visiting and they neither plan in advance or find a travel agent (which are free) to do so for them satisfactorily. Consequently they either become victims of false economy in their travel arrangements or they are gouged by expensive hotels and restaurants. You cannot transact important business when you are not in prime condition.

It pays off in health, comfort and success in business to be good to oneself. Your health and a clear brain are your capital assets in life. Be careful not to exhaust yourself during your work or recreation. This does not mean that you should not fling yourself with great zest into work and play but that you should not needlessly waste your energies. Anything that will add to your personal force and increase your vigor is worth its price. Spend generously for anything which will raise your achievement power and make you a more capable person.

The person who wants to do a fine piece of work, whether it be painting a picture or building a house, must have everything they need to work with in the best possible condition or the quality of his work will suffer. If you want to amount to anything you must regard your time as valuable and your energy as precious. You cannot afford to penny pinch with these resources.

Those who dissipate their energy are the worst kind of spendthrifts. Because they spend their time carelessly they can be thought of as suicides, intentionally killing their every chance in life. What use is ability to them if they cannot use it because their forces are weakened by false economics or wasted in daily trivia? What use is great intelligence, even genius, to one who is so physically weak that their energy becomes exhausted with the least effort?

To be confronted by a great opportunity which you are powerless to take advantage of or to feel that you cannot seize your great chance with assurance and vigor, is one of the most disheartening experiences that can ever come to a human being.

If you want to make the most of yourself get rid of everything which saps your vitality and hampers your ability to work. Do not drag around with a body that is half dead. Do not do anything, do not touch any Job which will lower your reserve of energy or lessen your chances of advancement.

Always ask yourself,: What is there in this job I am going to do that will add to my life's work, increase my potential, and keep me in condition to do my best?

Do not waste your precious energy in fretting, worrying, fault-finding, or little frictions and annoyances which accomplish nothing and merely make you irritable, cripple your personality and exhaust your energy. Look back over yesterday (even the last few hours) and see where your energy went. See how much of it you expended on trivia. You may have lost more energy in a fit of temper than in doing a normal day's work.

Some people are very careful to keep their pianos in tune but they never trouble themselves about the human instruments in their home which are out of tune most of the time. They try to play on jangled nerves and wonder why they produce discordant notes instead of harmonies.

The trouble with most of us is that we do not appreciate enough the beauty and complexity of the human mechanism or the potential of the being that dwells within it. We do not realize our powers and possibilities. We lose sight of our abilities. We live in our animal senses instead of rising through them to perfection. We do not dare to aspire to greatness or accomplishment.

The great aim of our lives should be to make every occasion an opportunity for achievement. Conserve your energies and guard your health.

Only if you take care of yourself can you expect to take care of the world.

Chapter 2

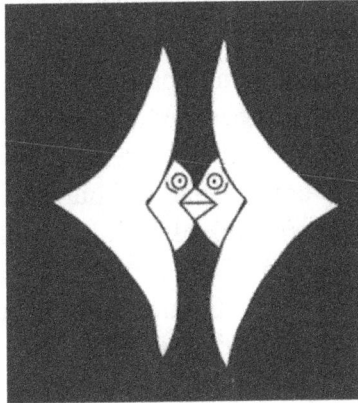

False Economizing

Long ago a Paris bank clerk went through the streets of the city carrying a bag of money. He dropped a ten-franc piece and it rolled from the sidewalk. The poor man set his bag down to look for the lost coin and while he was trying to extricate it from the gutter someone came up behind him and ran away with his bag of money. I have seen a woman spoil a fine pair of gloves trying to rescue a quarter which had fallen into the mud.

I knew a rich man who became such a slave to the habit of economizing (formed when he was trying to get a start in the world) that he very often lost ten dollars worth of valuable time trying to save one. This man, although wealthy, tore off the unused half-sheets of correspondence, cut out the backs of envelopes for scratch paper and was constantly spending time trying to save in little ways without regard for the time thus consumed. He carried the same spirit of miserly economy into his business. He forced his employees into petty savings like making them save used envelops as a matter of principle, etc.

True economy means the wisest expenditure of our resources considered from the broadest standpoint.

Comparatively few people have a healthy view of what real saving or economy means. I know a young man in business for himself who has lost many opportunities for advancement and a large amount of business by false economy in dress and stinginess about personal expenditures. He believes that there is something slightly unrespectable about a brand new suit of clothes. He would never think of inviting a customer or prospective client to lunch or of offering to pay his carfare if he happened to be travelling with him. He has such a reputation for being stingy that people do not like to do business with him. False economy has cost this man much. Many people injure their health seriously by trying to save money. If you are ambitious to do your best then beware of savings that will ultimately cost you too much. Multitudes of people are handicapped for years by constant nervous headaches which are simply due to eye-strain. They often have some slight defect in the lens of the eyes which causes a great deal of suffering and which can be corrected by glasses. But because of mistaken ideas of economy or vanity many people delay getting glasses.

I knew a man in business who periodically lost a considerable amount of time through neglect of his feet. Every step he took pained him yet he could not bear the idea of paying money to a foot doctor and submitting to a simple operation. Finally, after years of suffering, the operation was performed and it gave him immediate relief.

Many people delay some needed trivial surgery or dental operation for months or even years simply because they dread the expense and thus suffer not only a great deal of unnecessary pain but also bad effects on their careers. Make it a life principle never to delay the remedy of anything which is retarding your health or keeping you down. What a fearful amount of time and precious energy is wasted in most lives through false ideas of economy!

Some people will waste many dollars worth of valuable time and suffer much discomfort in visiting numerous stores looking for bargains and trying to save a few cents on some small purchase they wish to make. They will buy wearing apparel of inferior material because the price is low even though they know the articles will not wear well.

There are many ways that bargain hunters become victims of false economy. Because they are cheap they buy a great many things they do not actually need solely because their price seemed irresistible. Then they will pride themselves on how much money they have saved. If they would count up what they spend in a year they would generally find that they spend more than they would have if they bought what they actually wanted when they needed it and paid the regular price for it. So they wind up spending the same money and ending up with a inferior product.

Many people have a mania for attending auctions and buying goods which do not match anything else they have. The result is that their homes are veritable nightmares of bad taste. They never get the first best wear of anything. Their second-hand purchases are often just on the point of breaking down and constantly need repairing. Foolish buying is the worst kind of extravagance.

Quality and durability should be your first considerations in buying anything for constant use. Yet may people keep themselves poor by buying cheap articles which do not last.

There are plenty of people who would never throw away 50 cents but who would not hesitate to throw a dollar's worth of good food into the garbage pail. It is a strange fact that people who are close and stingy with their money are often extremely liberal with what the money will buy when it is food. In their estimation the value of food is determined by how much volume you can buy for a dollar.

P.T. Barnum once said, "Economy is not meanness. True economy consists in always making the income exceed the outgo." Most people fail to see this so they fail to do their best work because they do not consider what is most important to them. They do not keep their goals and their capacities in view. They handicap the potential of their outgo and destroy their greater opportunities by keeping their eyes fixed on petty savings.

Many people also strangle their chances without realizing it because they have psychologically become slaves to this habit of economizing in their expenditures. I have watched for some time the decay of a skyscraper erected years ago under contract. The owners dickered with a great many builders and finally let the contract go to the lowest bidder. The original estimate of cost, made by a reliable builder, was cut by a hundred thousand dollars. One may suppose that the estimate was for decent building. The actual building constructed has been a source of anxiety to the owners ever since its erection. Everything about it is cheap shoddy and rickety. Almost everyday something is out of order somewhere. The walls crack, the floors settle, the doors warp, and the windows stick. There is constant trouble with the cheap elevators and the heating. The boilers and all the machinery are frequently out of order. In the winter the building is cold because of poor insulation. The pipes leak because the pluming joints are poor and the furnishings are constantly being damaged. As a consequence the occupants got disgusted and moved out. Although the building is located where rents are high it cannot keep reliable tenants very long because they become exasperated. As a result the building attracts unreliable people. Financial losses in rents, constant repairs, the rapid deterioration of the building itself to say nothing of the wear and tear on the nervous system of the owners will be greater than the amount saved by the cheap contract.

No greater delusion ever entered a businessman's head than the idea that cheap labor is economy. Trying to cut the payroll down to the lowest possible dollar has ruined many a concern. Businessmen who have been successful have found that the best employees, like the best materials, are the most economical in the end. Breakage, losses in shipping, expensive blunders, the injury of merchandise, and loss of customers through employing cheap labor— these are not compensated for by low wages. Cheap labor means a poor product and a poor reputation. It means inferiority all along the line. The institution run by mediocre help is cheapened and attracts an inferior patronage.

Many a hotel has deteriorated because the proprietor tried to save a few thousand dollars a year by hiring cheap clerks, cooks, and waiters and by buying cheap food. Just that little difference between poor and excellent help between stale and fresh food has made the fortune of many shrewd hotels.

Some people never get out of the world of pennies into the world of dollars. They work so hard to save that they lose the larger gain in financial returns plus they miss the rich experience that comes from doing things right.

Almost everywhere today we see people wearing formal clothes and staying at cheap noisy hotels and motels and sleeping on uncomfortable beds. They are riding for days in cramped positions in cars in order to save the price of air fare and practicing all sorts of savings when they can afford better. Everyone must realize that you often have to pay for the good food, refreshing sleep, and cheerful recreation which enable you to have a clear brain and level head.

You cannot think efficiently with an over-taxed brain in an abused body.

People who as a rule accomplish a lot in a day and who are able to withstand great strain are usually good to themselves. When they travel they patronize the best hotel that they can afford and they eat the most nourishing (not necessarily the most expensive) food that they can possibly obtain. They make themselves as comfortable as possible especially in travelling and the result is that they are always in the best possible condition to do business.

Of course those who haven't the money cannot always afford the greatest comfort and efficiency but most people overestimate the value of their savings in comparison with their physical well-being. Judicious expenditure can greatly aid us in our ambitions, make a good impression and secure us quick recognition to help us gain promotion. Today great emphasis is placed on appearances. Success is not wholly a matter of merit even in an age of casual dress and informal socializing and living. Appearances have much to do with one's prospects and chances especially in large cities. In a small town, of course, everyone will soon know you and can quickly judge your ability and real worth yet even there the appearance of material success counts for a great deal.

Even more than your appearance is your associates which can affect your success in life. If you are in business for yourself you should cultivate the acquaintance of other men and women in your field. In this way you will become known, develop a reputation in your line of business, and attract a larger clientele. Seek out the associations or clubs frequented by your fellows. Keep abreast of what is going on in your community. You can remain aloof from your peers but most people cannot afford the great loss of information and contacts that will result from staying away from professional societies.

The young person who wants to succeed must remember that little things are important. Friendliness and generosity of spirit usually are great aids to success. No one can make the most of himself or herself if they do not internally feel a positive attitude. When we take care of ourselves we radiate this healthy mental attitude. It is a great thing to be physically healthy and to maintain mental poise. Then we radiate this exuberance of life, enthusiasm, and buoyancy of spirit.

When we are good to ourselves, we find it easier to radiate warmth toward others.

A healthy body is able to withstand great amounts of hard work and withstand hard knocks as well. Did you ever reflect how the mere physical ability to withstand a long persistent strain has carried many people you have known through difficult situations and rough times when weaker people have crumbled?

Everywhere we see people who are afraid to spend a little money to enlarge themselves by travel or higher education. They may have the security of a little money in the bank but their mental capital is small. Others who were more ambitious have started with far less have outdistanced them in life and in wealth.

Nobody admires a barren personality, the narrow soul of one who does not invest in books and travel and who invests in things but not in one's self and whose highest ambition is to save so many dollars. You can always pick out the people who are so overanxious about small savings that they lose sight of desired goals. They lack that generosity and breadth which marks the mature and fully developed person. Many people of this sort are stifled in business all their lives because they never have learned the effectiveness of judicious liberality. They do not know that a liberal sowing means a liberal harvest. Knowledge of modern business methods, a large acquaintance, and a respectable position can accomplish nothing without generosity and daring.

Economy, in its broadest sense, involves judgment, levelheadedness and breadth of vision. Paradoxically the wisest economy often requires lavish expenditure because there may be thousands of dollars resting on the spending of hundreds. It sometimes means establishing a broad and generous administration and liberal spending.

Some of the best business people I know are generous almost to extravagance with their customers or in their dealings with people. They think nothing of spending a thousand dollars if they can see two thousand or five thousand coming back from it. Petty economizers, on the other hand, are two narrow in their views, too limited in their outlook, and too frugal in their expenditures to ever embark on large enterprises. They hold the penny so close to their eyes that it shuts out the dollar.

He that soweth sparingly shall also reap sparingly.

Chapter 3

Conservation of Energy

Consider the energy stored in a ton of coal. We get only a fraction of that energy when we convert it to electricity. To discover some way to prevent this fearful waste of energy is one of the great problems confronting scientists today. Yet just as extreme a waste of energy goes on in our use of our own powers. Often not more than one per cent of our efforts gets results. The rest of our energy is dissipated in many ways.

A young person starting out in life should feel an almost limitless supply of energy welling up within them. They usually feel it possible to achieve wonders with this energy. Yet often young people are appalled to find that with all their vitality they have produced scarcely enough light to illuminate their own way and have nothing left for the world. Those who might have boasted of their strength and felt confident of shedding a light that would dazzle the world stumble along in semi-darkness. The energy which should have been expended in achievement has somehow been lost on the way.

It is not the energy we expend that dwarfs our achievement and whittles away at life: it is what we foolishly throw away.

Millions of people have been disappointed in life by letting this precious energy slip away from them when they might have achieved wonders. We must learn not only how to conserve our energies, but when to expend them.

It is considered a terrible thing for a youth to throw away a thousand dollars of their father's hard earned money in a few wild evenings' dissipation; but far worse is the loss of their inner vitality, signalled by their poor sense of values, and the waste of their energy which would have been better expended in physical and mental achievement. What is the loss of money compared with the demoralization wrought by such behavior? Deterioration of one's values undermines the very foundation of all that is best in life.

It is not debauchery alone that robs us of energy. The wanton waste of energy in many daily activities might be spent in more fruitful pursuits. Some time ago, for instance, I watched a marathon bicycle race in which the contestants expended more energy than they would have in accomplishing years of ordinary work. The exhausted victims were determined not to give up the struggle even though they might die of overexertion. The drawn lines about the mouth and eyes and the haggard expressions of those people in the last hours of their desperate ride haunted everybody who saw them. Many of those naturally strong rugged bicyclists had to be lifted from their wheels while some of them fell prone upon the ground in their utter physical exhaustion.

It isn't merely that we turn even our most healthful and recreative exercises and sports into near fatalities; apparently we find it more easy to be single-mined and wholehearted in competitive sport than in life and business. Over devotion to sport reveals a lack of purpose in life.

A noted physician says that most people expend ten times the energy really necessary in almost everything that they do. They grasp a pen as if it were a crowbar, keep the muscles of the arm tense when they write and pour out as much energy in signing their names as an athlete would in throwing a heavy weight a great distance. Not one in hundred, he says, knows how to make proper use of their muscles or to relax perfectly when at rest.

It is chiefly through sleep or complete relaxation that we are able to store up energy. A normal person who knows how to sleep and relax is not nervous or restless. They have control of their muscles and are poised and self-possessed. They give the impression of great reserves of energy. Inadequate or poor rest is betrayed by one's gestures and the behavior of the eyes. Fidgeting, and inattentive gaze, and the inability to concentrate are all effects of tension and lack of sleep. People who get enough sleep are well balanced, even-tempered, and do not need artificial stimulants.

It is no wonder that so many of our nervous and over-active business people feel exhausted in the morning. They are tired most of the time and they resort to stimulants to keep up the intense unnatural strain and to give them artificial energy. Tired brains and nerves are responsible for many mistakes in business as well as fatal accidents, crimes of passion and suicides. A well-rested person is normal, strong and vigorous. They are not haunted by all sorts of unhealthy appetites or by a desire to do crazy things or to live an unnatural life of weird excitement and self-indulgence.

Make it your policy to look back over the day and see just where your energy has gone. How much of it has leaked away from you on trifles? Perhaps you have wasted it in fits of fuming, grumbling and fault-finding or in the little frictions that have accomplished nothing and merely left you exhausted. You may have expended more energy in a fit of bad temper than in your real work. Perhaps you did not realize that in going through your office or place of business like a mad bull loose in a china shop you destroyed your most important asset—your good relations with your fellow-workers. You turned on every faucet of your mental and physical reservoir and left them open until all your energy, stored up in the night before, had run off. When you look back over your days, see whether your criticizing and nagging has accomplished anything. You will find the answer is No. You only lost your energy and self-control, your self-respect and the respect and admiration of your associates.

When evening comes some people are unable to stay awake. During the day they did not balance and control their expenditure of energy and night finds them with every reservoir and water-main empty and an easy prey to illness or ill-temper. How pitiful it is to see such people anxiety-ridden before they reach thirty-five and looking old at forty not because of bad times and hard work but because of useless fretting and anxiety that have only prematurely aged them and brought discord into their homes.

Much of the worst dissipation of energy is not what is commonly called immoral. It is usually the result of ignorance, carelessness or neglect but it is dissipation all the same. A great deal of energy is wasted in working without a system in mind and in not seizing the right end of the thing at the start. On the other hand, many of us so completely exhaust our strength in useless anxiety by anticipating our tasks and mentally doing our work over and over again before we begin that we have no energy left for the actual work when we finally begin.

Some of us waste our energy and make our lives ineffective by trying to do too many things. The ability to do one complex thing superbly usually excludes the possibility of doing other complex things well. If we focus our attention on one complex thing it is necessarily withdrawn from everything else. The mind is unable to concentrate upon more than one complex thing at a time and concentration is necessary if we wish to excel.

People who are constantly making resolutions with great vigor and determination but who never put them into execution do not realize how much precious energy they waste in dreaming and wishing. They live in dreamland but do not make their dreams become real.

Everywhere we see young men and women unable to overcome the obstacles in their paths simply because they lack the energy to do so. It is pitiful to see many of them at work yawning and stretching all day, sleepy and unspontaneous, unenthusiastic and dull. They have thrown away their energy on a hundred trivialities and have nothing left to put into their work.

If you want to make your mark in the world and do your part in advancing civilization you must concentrate on the usefulness of your activities.

Chapter 4

Living Within Your Means

Despite the supposedly advanced state of today's society there still exists an insane rivalry among wealthy people to out-do one another in possessions and luxurious living. A wife who was suing for divorce a while ago maintained that a woman in her position required from thirty-five to forty thousand dollars a year for dress alone and that this was a comparatively small item in the cost of maintaining her household. Another New York socialite says that she spends from one hundred to one hundred and fifty thousand dollars a year on her wardrobe; that she has many dresses that cost a thousand dollars each and that her shoes cost outrageously.

The attitudes of such women may seem a far cry from those members of the middle class who aspire to swimming pools, more than two cars, fifty-two vacation week-ends in a year, etc. Yet there are obvious weaknesses in both sorts of self-indulgence and vanity. In serving the pleasure principle and catering to your vanity, you has little time left for the things that really matter—things we shall soon discuss.

It is helpful to recognize the influence of some of the rich upon the average unperceptive person who cannot afford luxurious living or dress. Not only much of the discontent and unhappiness in society but also a large part of the immorality and crime in countries are due to the frustrated desires of the poor and middle class to attain a material paradise that is constantly advertised by the business world in a consumer society.

The mere possession of money does not give one the right to poor values and gross waste. This is setting an example to one's fellows that is unsatisfactory. If average people feel that a certain amount of material comfort will give them a happy life and they are deluded into feeling that they must strain to keep up an appearance of wealth at the possible sacrifice of their integrity, then these people will never realize their happiness.

The marketplace will always offer far more than one can afford and promoters will always insist that you must buy their new products.

Some affluent people attempt to justify their extravagance on the grounds that it gives employment to many otherwise jobless people! No greater delusion ever crept into the human brain than the idea that wanton extravagance is justified on the grounds that it gives employment. The problems infinitely outweigh any possible good it may accomplish.

The vulgar flaunting of wealth is demoralizing to the rich, a temptation to the middle class and an aggravation to the poor. It excites members of all classes to pathetic attempts at maintaining the appearance of wealth. This attitude leads people to live unnatural and thereby often unhealthy lives. They often become abnormally selfish because they are completely absorbed is getting the most they can for themselves. They consequently think very little about others. They maintain expensive habits and manifest a passion for show.

A man who was rich once told me that he had no idea of marrying. By remaining single he could live like a prince, as he expressed it, keeping house where he liked, staying at the best hotels when he travelled, patronizing good tailors and taking an occasional trip abroad. If he married, on the other hand, he had to face the prospect of dividing his income with a family and he would be obliged to live in a poorer part of the city, in less luxury and ease. He could not begin to keep up the appearance of wealth or make the display which at that time he was able to afford. He said that women expect so much today that young men require a lot of courage to assume the responsibility of marriage.

His greed deprived him one of the great pleasures of live and that has no dollar value.

In this age when women as well as men bring home the bacon other problems have arisen to discourage young people from establishing families. The importance of the child in our lives has been greatly diminished which erodes our childhood fantasies and dreams. Also many men find it difficult to establish themselves in housekeeping and parenting roles on a share-and-share-alike basis with their mates. Some women require this if they are to be parents because they have taken on not only full-time job roles but professional commitments as well. In addition, the once sacred status of the home has been diminished. Tasks that once devoured the homemaker's time are now done by machines. The moral role the parent used to be expected to sustain is now handed over to the television in their home, instructors and teachers at school, and other organizers of their children's time. It is only natural that many women who are either organizers, intellectuals, artists, or leaders are applying their considerable skills in these roles— outside the home.

Ironically, such roles may teach women to curb their tastes for luxuries, even though initially such tastes spurred them on their desire to get out of the house. The women who steels herself against the extravagant temptations directed toward her sex by the advertising world can make a career for herself, choose to marry when and whom she wishes, and shape her own life. Running into debt to procure what one cannot afford only reveals one's basic insecurities.

Years ago it used to be considered a disgrace for a person to be in debt unless he or she were in business for themselves or there were some other justification for it. Now it is common to see people with small salaries heavily in debt— for luxuries. Never has there been such a perfect mania among all classes to keep up appearances as exists today. Everywhere we see people toiling to keep in the social swim, struggling to break into the stratum above them, staining every nerve to do things that they cannot afford to do, simply because others do them.

It is interesting to note how often secretaries dress like daughters of the rich, millionaires' daughters wear blue jeans, and clerks dress better then their employers. In a world where so many are trying to appear to be better off than they are it is impossible to judge correctly by appearances. Background and skills ought to count more to your future employer than appearance.

Not long ago a woman of great organizational skills and daring in business, who contributed much to her firm and was well-rewarded with high pay and extra benefits, nearly lost her home because she was addicted to spending money. Although this example exhibits a private neurosis, it shares certain causes with the social disease of keeping up with the Joneses. There are plenty of people in all our large cities who do not allow themselves enough to eat, who scrimp and cut corners at home for the sake of keeping up appearances in the world. What terrible inconvenience, hardship, and suffering we endure on account of other people's opinions! What fools we make of ourselves, scheming and contriving to present inflated images of our lives and personalities. Worrying about other people's opinions makes us unhappy and discontented. We should not enslave ourselves to false appearances. How stupid it is to discard our clothes, for example, not because they are badly worn but because others will think it strange that we do not wear new clothes all the time. It is equally foolish to set about acquiring the goods which proclaim security and status to the world before security and status are truly ours. The effect of all this deception in living and in dress is to contributive to the mediocrity of the average person; it implies a superficiality of character and a lack of genuineness contradictory to our original claims before the world. How can you respect yourself if you are living in luxury which you cannot afford?

Trying to make people believe that you are better off than you really are is a boomerang which strikes back with a fatal rebound. It is impossible for you to pretend to be one thing when you are another. Do not deceive yourself into thinking that good clothes or a palatial home can make a man or a woman. The display of lavish wealth, pretended or real, is an exhibition of bad taste. Living honestly affords the greatest satisfaction in life.

Those who know how to achieve serenity in their lives, no matter how complex the roles they play, achieve it by reserving for themselves a private life suited to their own desires and needs, rather than the need to appear a certain way before others. Not long ago I was visited by a dear friend who has the courage to live a simple life in the midst of the pyrotechnics of social life in a big city The man, who has little capital, has a strong character and a sweet personality. He envies no one, bows to no one and he is wonderfully independent. He walks like a conqueror. He has no anxiety about the future. He lives a full complete life as he goes along. The moment one enters his atmosphere one is conscious of being in the presence of a rich personality. It does not require as much courage as you might think to live the life you can afford.

"Paint me as I am, warts and all, or 1 will not pay you for

the picture" exclaimed Oliver Cromwell to the painter who was smoothing his rough features in a portrait. This is the sort of honesty that is sorely needed today.

All people owe it to themselves to live a real life, whether they be rich or poor; to be, and not merely to seem. We owe it to ourselves to be genuine.

Chapter 5

Take A Vacation

To me the meanest flower that blooms can give
Thoughts that do often lie too deep for tears.
- Wordsworth

The woods were filled so full with song
There seemed no room for sense of wrong.
- Tennyson

Few people taking their summer vacations realize the opportunities before them for education as well as pleasure in rest and relaxation. "The greatest thing a human soul ever does in this world", said a famous nature lover, "is to see something and tell what he saw in a plain way." Think how much would be added to your life if you were able to see things as this great nature lover saw them. To him beauty and harmony were everywhere. Does it seem ridiculous that this critic and essay-ist who would go into ecstasies over the structure of a leaf or flower or over the scale of a fish or a grain of sand could not afford the time to lecture for five hundred dollars a night? To study the wonders of Nature, to hear her music and interpret her language were riches enough for him "The more we see of beauty everywhere", said another naturalist, "in Nature, in life, in man and child, in work and rest, in the outward and inward world,— the more we see perfection of nature or God." If we love Nature and study her, we cannot help seeing the beauty of order everywhere and it will make us stronger and happier.

For most people one of the greatest joys of life comes from having their faculties and senses awake and responsive to Na-ture. It is criminal to allow a child to grow up without learning to use their eyes and ears properly. Children should be trained to see and hear things as they are.

One of the first lessons that should be impressed on every child, whether living in the city or in the country, is that of properly viewing objects out of doors. If children learn this they will become not only more sensitive people but persons of broader education and culture and they are more likely to turn out happy and successful.

At the cost of a few hundred dollars the poorest city child may be given a stay in the wilderness. Many art lovers travel across continents to view the works of the great masters and give fortunes to possess a canvas or two representing land-scapes but few of them are real appreciators of Nature's picture gallery which cost nothing.

Many of us have become so self-absorbed and have had our attention so long focused upon our material goals and careers that we are unable to direct our faculties outward except upon our immediate concerns and interests. To learn to see things out of doors would be, to many of us, like learning a new profes-sion or occupation in middle life.

We often see a weary or broken-down urbanite go to the

wilderness for rest and recuperation only to return to their city home or office unrefreshed and unstimulated. They were unable to enjoy any of the country's wonder and beauty. They were not in sympathy with the voices of Nature and could not hear them. They had become absorbed in the pursuit of wealth and could no longer respond to Nature's appeals. They had eyes, but saw not. They had ears but heard not. They had voice, but spoke not. And so they continue to miss the real wealth and joy of life. How different life might be for them had they been able to experience and express the joys described by Emerson:

Whoso inhabiteth the wood,
And chooseth light, wave, rock and bird,
Before the money-loving herd,—
Into such a forrester shall pass,
From his companions, power and grace.
Pure shall he be without, within,
From the old adhering sin;
He shall never be old
Nor his fate shall be foretold;
He shall watch the speeding year
Without wailing, without fear;
He shall be happy in his love,
Like to like shall joyful prove.

People uncover their head and bow in reverence when they enter the sacred cathedrals of Europe. One need not travel far, however, to be renewed in spirit by the bounty of Nature. No matter how jaded or irritable we may be when we go to the wilderness, our mood soon changes. We feel as though we were drinking in the nectar of the gods. Every breath is a tonic and every sight a rest for the weary mind.

There is a spirit in Nature to which we respond. It is expressed in plants—in flowers, in grasses, in trees; in meadows and mountains; in the sky and in the song of birds. It touches our very soul and puts us in tune with the Infinite, to use the vocabulary of Wordsworth, bringing us into harmony with the great Spirit which pervades the universe. There is a magical restorative power in the spirit which breathes in the wilderness and it is a power which heals and refreshes. Who has not felt the magic of recreation, refreshment, and rejuvenation within them when they are walking in the wilderness? We can actually feel ourselves being made over, we can actually sense the renewing process going on within us when we are in the world of Nature - despite the worries, frictions and discords of contemporary life. Even if we have wrecked our nervous systems we feel the magic.

How insignificant we find the things which yesterday forced us to distraction! We feel as though we had taken a new lease on life. The person who comes back from a vacation of this sort is often a much better person than the one who went away. I have seen the most nervous and people completely transformed by a few weeks in the country or in the wild. They had an entirely different outlook on business and life in general. The things that had irritated and worried them before the vacation they took in stride when they returned. They were new creatures and born again.

There is no doubt that this rejuvenation, this feeling of refreshment, comes from the fundamental nature of our being and is the cure for most of the hurts in our world. Vacationing in the wild provides not only a break from the usual hierarchy of routine tasks but a complete change of scene. By inviting eye and ear to be more perceptive of beauty Nature awakens faculties in us which can continue to be delighted during a walk in the city park or by the river or ocean shore. Sensitivity to the weather, seasonal changes and those glimpses of the natural panorama which the city can provide is heightened by the trip to the wild.

Great minds have always felt the peculiar healing power of Nature; why should we be ashamed to be sensitive to the divine current of life found in the wilderness? Visit it often.

Chapter 6

The Importance of Play

"What makes you Americans hurry so?", asks a distin-guished foreign visitor to our country, "This is not living, it is merely existing."

We Americans lead lives that are, as a rule, too mundane. We treat our work as a game in deadly earnest and work hard at our play. We give ourselves little time to reflect upon our lives, our work, and our personal relationships. Frequently we hand a small amount of time over to professionals in the belief that the integration of our personalities can be accomplished by a psy-chiatrist, minister, priest, or other director. When we indulge in introspection it is as a neurosis or task and we do not make use of the precious revelations which our brief encounters with Nature and ourselves provide. For this reason, we fail to inte-

grate ourselves into the world. To the citizens of other nations
we sometimes appear to be over-worked like machinery run at
forced speed which squeaks for lack of oil.

For some of us the habit of hurrying has become almost
a disease. Because we have become accustomed to a furious
pace during our work hours we find it difficult to slow down, to
unwind, even when there is no need to hurry. Our movements,
habits, and manners give us the appearance of always being in
a rush even when we are on vacation.

Many people do not seem to know how to let themselves
go. The ghost of worry or anxiety is nearly always present to
mar their enjoyment and keep them from play.

*We fear that it would not he dignified for adults to act like
children.*

For these reasons many people are prevented from getting the best out of their recreation. Such persons could learn
a good lesson from the healthful abandon of young cattle and
colts turned out to pasture in the spring. How they kick up their
heels, as though delighting in sheer existence!

Many a harried business person ignores the most obvious
seasonal changes unless their commute homeward to the sub-
urbs shows them to their senses. Cities today are far from what
we know they can be. There are sections in most large cities
where tenement windows frame no view of trees and where the
commercial areas are unrelieved by landscaping or recreation
areas and only an empty lot performs the function of a city
park.

American urbanization in the last century saw the destruction of natural recreation areas in and close to the city. The
focus on industrial progress and the lack of city planning as
we know it today was responsible for the disappearance of a
stream-side and forest. The private gardens and city parks, both
inside the city proper and on its perimeter, are scarce.

The changing face of the city was then reflected our social
changes. The variety of entertainments increased, sports flour-

ished and professionalism began. Recreation itself began to be regarded as a necessary part of modern living. Twentieth-century preoccupations with the proper use of leisure time have led to the phenomenon of publicly funded and organized recreation on the municipal, state and federal levels. Private and corporate entertainment caters to a wide variety of tastes and entertainment has become big business.

Notwithstanding the fact that rural life has the natural advantages of pure air, stimulating vistas, fresh food, and freedom from the noise and pollution of the city, urbanites can frequently appear to be more cheerful than those who live far from the madding crowd. This may be in part because they have so many more facilities for amusement at their disposal. People who live in congested areas feel the need for amusement and they are hungry for fun. They live under strong pressures and take advantage of the opportunities for easing the strain of their lives which the city creates. From symphonies to the theatre to movies, no matter how superficial or light or frivolous, entertainment in the city is usually well patronized. The city affects the passions and emotions, assaults the senses and evokes response. That is why nothing is more dreadful than loneliness in the city. There is something grotesque about an unsolitary loneliness in the city. Suburbanites, who lead the most comfortable of lives must beware of the dangers of a way of life constructed solely for ease. Neither the advantages of rural life or the advantages of the city are theirs unless they actively seek them out. What most people need in their daily lives is more relief from the tedium of work throughout their day. Do not allow an artificial work situation to keep you from laughing out loud or from giving yourself up with abandon to your fun-loving instincts.

A cheerful disposition that can laugh in the face of disaster and be impervious to insult and injury. It is a divine gift.

To be able to laugh away trouble is a greater fortune than the greatest riches.

It is a fortune that is within the reach of all who have the courage to hope for the best by saying, "Courage, friend, the devil is dead!" To ignorant superstitious people the devil is very much alive. He has the whisk of his tail in all the amusements. Always take it for granted that you are beyond the power of the devil to harm. Remember that laughter can banish evil. Storytellers and jokesters have a faculty for self-refreshment which retards old age. It seems that people who seldom laugh, people who cannot appreciate a joke, age much faster.

An aging person ought to be serene and calm and purged of all the agitations of youth. In our stereotypical view a sweet dignity, a quiet repose, and a calm expression should characterize those who have had all that was richest and best in the age in which they lived but quite the contrary is often seen. Recently I watched an old man in a restaurant who was so nervous that he could scarcely eat. He was constantly drumming on the table with his fingers, dropping things, twitching his elbows and his knees and moving his feet. He was drinking the strongest coffee imaginable in order to quiet his nerves. It really was pitiful to see this old man fidgeting as though he had some disease, deprived of the serenity of his years and his share of physical dignity and poise.

Frequently we hear that the lives of the urban elderly are beset with the anxieties that come from younger generations. The break-down of the extended family and inadequate retirement financing contribute to the anxieties of those whom society should most earnestly protect. The elderly, especially those who relied on their work community for social needs, have a greater need for group recreation than they often recognize.

Our criteria for evaluating ourselves is frequently social. When our community is diminished our feeling of self-worth is diminished. The development of new interests or the simple enjoyment of group activities in which leadership qualities and social expertise are called once more into play build up feelings of self-worth and usefulness in retired persons threatened by unstructured leisure.

Half the misery in the world might be avoided if people would make a business of having plenty of fun at home instead of running everywhere else in search of it. The happy home is the result of conscious effort.

In a happy home you can almost see a sign over the door that says:. *Now for Rest and Fun. No Business Troubles Allowed Here.*

This is a good home building motto. Whatever your lot in life give joy to your home. Joy heals where sorrow, worry, jealousy, envy and bad temper create friction and grind away at the delicate machinery of the human brain.

When you have had a discouraging day, when everything seems to have gone wrong and you arrive home exhausted and depressed, instead of making your home miserable by going over your bad day detach yourself from your troubles and trials and revel in your family. In other words, rather than dragging your business home and making yourself and your family unhappy lock all your worries in your office. Do not be like a man I know who casts such gloom over his whole family that he spoils the peace of his home life. His wife and children almost dread to see him come home. Resolve that your family will have a home of pleasant memories and secure relationships. If you abandon your business worries when you go home at night you will be surprised to see how professional wrinkles are ironed out and disappointment put into perspective in the morning.

Make it your business to establish a home where every member of your family can be happy. Fill it with bright cheerful music. Physicians employ music for the same reason the supermarkets and answering services do, it drives away irritations and soothes the nerves. Music can do more than soothe. Music can restore and preserve mental harmony. Some nervous diseases are wonderfully helped by good music. Music keeps the mind off one's troubles and gives Nature a chance to heal all sorts of mental discord.

Among the many things that you can do to instill joy in the rhythm of your day nothing will give you more satisfaction than the deliberate enjoyment of family life. You will find that a little fun in the evening romping around will make you sleep more easily. You may also be surprised to see how rested you are the next day. You may also be surprised to see how much more work you can do and how much more readily you can employ yourself in your daily tasks when you have a certain amount of innocent fun each day.

We have all experienced the lift which comes from a good time at home or with friends, especially when we have come home after a hard exacting day's work. When we are mentally fatigued and exhausted, what magic a single hour's fun will often accomplish! How a little frivolity releases us from weariness and how the thrill of laughter invites joy into one's whole being! Laughter is as natural a form of expression as speech. It is carried over into music, art, or work of any kind. We cannot really be healthy without a certain amount of it. We cannot enjoy our work without the play of our wits or without a break of some sort with which to relieve tedium.

There is something abnormal about a parent who is annoyed by the romping and laughter of children. The probabilities are that their own high spirits were suppressed in their childhood. The person who does not want to grow old psychologically must keep in touch with the young.

Do not be afraid of playing in the home or of getting down on the floor and romping with the children. Never mind your clothes, the carpets, or the furniture. Just determine that you will put a lot of good fun into your life everyday, come what may.

Do not be overly solemn at the table. It is a place for laughter and joking and for bright repartee. Swallow a lot of fun with your meals. It is the best thing in the world for your health. Dinner time ought to be anticipated by everyone in the family as an occasion for a good time, for hearty laughter, and for bright entertaining conversation. Children should be trained to abandon their quarrels when they come to the table and to take advantage of the opportunity for family conversation. Happy family dinners would revolutionize homes, mitigate against the breakdown of the family, and drive away the doctors.

I know a family whose dinner hour is characterized by light repartee and humor and it is a real joy to dine with them. There is rivalry among all the members of the family to see who can say the brightest and wittiest thing or tell the best stories. There is no apparent nagging in this family. A few hours of sunshine will do for plants what months of cloudy weather cannot. It is the sunshine that gives the health and vitality to fruit and flower.

We all require mental sunshine.

I have been in homes that were so somber and gloomy that they made me feel depressed the moment I entered them. Nobody dared to call their soul their own. To laugh out loud was regarded almost as a misdemeanor. If the children made any noise they were silenced. Everybody who attempted to have a little fun was promptly squelched. One felt the presence of an invisible sign posted everywhere about the house: "No joking, romping or playing allowed here. Laughter is forbidden. Life is too short and too serious for such frivolity. Besides, the furniture might be scratched, things might be broken, or the children's clothes soiled or rumpled."

A little while ago I was the guest of a household where the mother was the nervous fretful sort who neither enjoys herself or lets others enjoy themselves. Her family was quite large and scarcely five minutes passed during my stay when the poor thing was not correcting, scolding or nagging one of her children. It did not seem to matter what they were doing, she would tell them not to do it. If a child stood in an open doorway or near an open window she was sure he would catch a horrible cold. The child must not eat this, they must not do that, they must not make noise, they must not play. On into the evening she kept scoulding her children in this manner until they were nervous and fretful. The result of this constant suppression is that there is not a really normal child in the family. There is a sort of hungry unsatisfied look on everyone of their faces. They give one the impression that they long to get away from their mother and that they need to indulge in unrestrained laughter and yearn to play to their heart's content.

It is worse than cruel to annihilate any childhood and to suppress the fun-loving instinct which is as natural as breathing, in any child. No wealth or luxury in later life can compensate for the loss of one's childhood.

We have all seen children who have had no childhood. Whether they have been repressed and forbidden to do this for so long that they have lost the faculty of having a good time or because they have been given adult responsibilities in childhood. Our heart goes out to them..

Unfortunate indeed is the home that is not illuminated by at least one cheerful, bright, sunny young face. A home that does not ring with the persistent laughter and merry voice of a child. Children should be allowed to remain children as long as possible. Ask yourself the question: "What has responsibility, seriousness, or sadness to do with childhood?" We always feel indignant as well as sad when we see evidence of precocious maturity, over seriousness care or anxiety in a child's face for we know that someone has done something wrong here.

Little ones should be kept strangers to anxiety, overly reflective thoughts, and subjective moods. Their lives should be kept bright and buoyant, cheerful and full of sunshine. They should be encouraged to laugh, to play, and to romp to their hearts' content. The serious side of life will come only too quickly, do what we may to prolong childhood.

The first duty we have towards a child is that of teaching it to express its inborn gladness and joy with as much freedom as the bird that makes the whole meadow glad with its song.

Laughter, absolute abandon, freedom, and security in parental affection are essential to its health and later success. These are part of a child's natural state. Their childhood cannot be considered normal without them.

Suppression of the fun-loving aspect of a child's nature ultimately entails the suppression of their mental growth.

There is every evidence in a child's nature that play is as necessary to its normal complete development as food. It is as necessary as sunshine is to the perfect development of a plant. A childhood without play is a childhood that has no budding and flowering.

The partial unfolding of its petals only indicates poor fruit.

The necessity for play in the early stages of a child's development is argued by the strength of the play instinct in all young life, including that of the entire animal kingdom.

Play provides the exercise by which the physical being is perfected in strength and skill. In addition the child at play is stimulated emotionally to heights of exuberance and fellowship and experiences a release from the cares of the adult world around him. They can explore, achieve success, invent and role play without fear. Socialization is something that naturally occurs through group play and can be a potentially therapeutic exercise for the child because they can be creative in the dramatic invention of external roles which helps to rid themselves of trauma. Someone has pointed out that play is both preparation for life and one of the chief realizations of life.

Playfulness is manifest in the most exquisite music humans have ever produced, as well as in the arts, literature and drama. It is an expression of the satisfaction and joy of the artist in their own power and growth and in their medium. All areas of human endeavour are enlivened by a sense of play. In a way, there is nothing more ludicrous than the spectacle of an adult who takes their sport so seriously that it loses all recreative value.

Most homes are far too serious. Why not let the children

dance and play to their hearts content? They will get knocked about enough in the world later and they will see enough of the rough side of life all too soon. Let's agree that they shall at least be as happy as you can make them while at home so that if they should have any unfortunate experiences later they can look back upon their home as a sweet oasis in their life and the happiest place on earth.

Let children give vent to all that is joyous and happy in their nature and they will blossom into helpful men and women. Spontaneity, buoyancy, and the bubbling over of animal spirits are attractive personal qualities in men and women in business. A cheerfulness that is born of confidence in one's self and one's world is frequently the result of a decidedly happy childhood—not one free from all adversity, perhaps, but one essentially blessed by parental love. Buoyant people are more likely to be happy in any profession or walk in life than those who are inflexible. They persist in the face of difficulties which discourage those who have been suppressed and denied freedom and responsibility.

Generally, only happy children continue to be happy adult citizens. You cannot give children too much love. They thrive on affection as well as fun and the home is the place above all others where they should get an abundance of both. Someone has said that if you want to ruin your children let them think that all mirth and enjoyment must be left on the threshold when they come home at night. When one regards the home as merely a place in which to eat, drink, and sleep, the result is the degradation of one's self, one's work, and one's personal relationships.

Children should be taught the art of getting enjoyment out of the common things in life. This will prevent the development of habitual restlessness and discontent and the disposition of always thinking that one would be happier if only they were somewhere else in other circumstances.

Again, if you want your children to be well, strong, and

happy, try to cultivate in them as much as possible a sense of humor and an instinct for fun. Teach children to laugh at their misfortunes and to see the ludicrous aspect of unpleasant experiences which cannot be avoided or ignored. The tonic of fun promotes healing; it is a cure-all for our emotional bruising.

In adults, all our faculties are dependent upon our inner equilibrium—balance, harmony—call it what you will. If we are unhappy, our efficiency is seriously impaired. Discouragement, worry, anxiety, fear and anything abnormal in our experience affects not only our private lives but our professional lives as well.

By the same token, whatever tends to encourage us or to brighten hope and bring good cheer multiplies our efficiency. There is no other single thing which so buoys up one's spirits and refreshes the whole person as play and innocent fun. The enormous success of the entertainment world is due largely to its ability to satisfy the basic human need for amusement. The participation in group sport, games or conversation more fully indulges the spirit of play in our recreation.

When the demand for amusement is satisfied and the need for play is gratified the whole person is improved, enlarged, and invigorated. The human machine quickly becomes more healthy and more efficient. When the need for play is repressed or denied a famine in the personality is experienced which is emotional, intellectual and, ultimately, ethical. Much of the morbidity of the present age and of its tastes is due to the stifled childhoods of precocious adults. The joy of childhood keeps everything within us sweet. It evaporates worry, jealousy, and the explosive passions just as sunshine evaporates a morning mist. A joy within keeps us from becoming soured on exterior life. On the other hand a pessimistic crotchety disposition, a faultfinding, finicking, disagreeable mind sours everything is life. Without the sun of optimism projects do not thrive or ripen just as fruit does not become sweet in the dark. Perhaps because the tendency of pessimism is to distort, what makes us happiest also makes us more efficient. If joy abides in any one expression it is in laughter. The habit of frequent and hearty laughter will not only save you many a doctor's bill it will also save you years of life. Laughter is a foe to pain and disease, a sure cure for the blues. Be cheerful, and you will improve your own surroundings by making everyone around you happier and healthier. Laughter keeps the heart young and enhances physical beauty.

Laughter and good cheer promote the love of life and the love of life is half of health.

Every child is going to have a confidant, someone to whom they can tell their secrets and whisper the hopes and ambitions they would not breathe to others. We take it for granted that their mother will be closer to them than any other person, in many ways, but every child will have some male friend who will stand in a unique relation of advisor and confidant to them. This friend should be their father. You cannot afford to have your children feel that you are indifferent to them.

Many parents do not realize the importance of little things in a child's life. Do not think that you can be too busy to tell the children how to fly their kites, kick a ball, make toys, or play their games. Do not deny them the pleasure of your company in their games. If you begin early enough it will be comparatively easy for you to gain your child's confidence. From infancy, children should grow up knowing that you care for them in a special way and they should know that you, their parent, are personally interested in their well-being and happiness.

Any business person would be horrified at the suggestion that they might ruin their child by neglect or that absorption in business affairs would result in the undoing of their child. Yet it is very easy to forfeit a child's confidence. It will take only a little snubbing and scolding, a certain amount of indifference, unkind criticism, nagging and unreasonableness to shut off forever any intimacy between you and your child.

One of the bitterest things in many business people's lives

has been the discovery after they have made their money, that they have lost the affections of their children. They would give large portions of their fortunes to recover their loss.

Some parents constantly nag, find fault, and never think of praising their children or expressing any appreciation of their work or efforts. Children thrive on praise. This is why many of them think more of one parent or another—because one parent is more considerate more appreciative, more affectionate and does not hesitate to praise them when they do well.

I know a man who takes great pains to keep the confidence of a pet dog. He would not think of whipping or scolding the dog because he would not risk losing its affection but he is always scolding his boy. He finds fault with everything his son does, criticizes his conduct and his associates, and tells him that he will never amount to anything. What chance has a boy to grow or to develop the best that is in him in such an atmosphere?

There is nothing so encouraging to a child, especially if they find it difficult to do what is right, as genuine appreciation. It establishes confidence between parent and child and thus helps establish and keep open the avenues of communication essential for any good relationship. You should regard the confidential relation between yourself and your child as one of the most precious things in your life and you should never take the chance of forfeiting it. It costs something to keep it but it is worth everything to you and your child.

I never knew a child who regarded their parents as their best friends and who did not need to keep any secrets from them go very far wrong in life.

Chapter 7

Lies

In one of his stories Mark Twain says of a character that whatever statement the character chose to make was entitled to a prompt and unquestioning acceptance as a lie.

There are a great many kinds of liars and a great many ways of lying. Someone once undertook to classify lies. He distinguished lies of vanity; lies of flattery; lies of convenience; lies of interest; lies of fear; lies of malignity; lies of malevolence, and lies of wantonness. Mark Twain counts eight hundred and sixty-nine varieties of lies.

We all know foolish liars who lie without motive from force of habit. We can understand a person's lying in some situations but to lie without any purpose whatever seems to the normal mind an unintelligible thing and to lie unscrupulously to the harm of others is contemptible to all.

A very large class of liars are liars of carelessness and thoughtlessness—people who did not mean to lie but who are slipshod in their mental processes. Their observation is faulty and they do not see or hear with exactitude. They do not take pains to get the exact facts about anything that goes into their head. One of the most unfortunate circumstances in business is caused by such sloppiness in thinking. Those who we would otherwise trust we cannot trust because they are never right.

The most pernicious liar to have as a companion is the one who deliberately lies or distorts the truth to the detriment of others. Whether a flatterer or a slanderer (and the same person can be both), once they are found out such a person can never again be trusted. They have neither a regard for human integrity, for truth itself or for the precious thing that is one's reputation.

The flatterer cannot bear to wound you in your weak points but feels no scruples in chopping you down to size when you are not present. The polite liar dodges and deceives in order to be courteous. He would rather lie than tell you unwelcome truths. There are liars who cannot bear to tell the truth when it reflects upon themselves or does not flatter their vanity. These liars may be believed in anything which does not reflect on themselves or put them in an unfavorable light.

So-called benevolent liars often escape condemnation because their motives appear to be good. A good-natured woman or man, compelled to dismiss an employee, will sometimes give an undeserved recommendation quite unconscious of the injury thus done a later employer.

Slander, the worst brand of falsehood, does not always require a lying tongue. A person may lie by his silence when it is his duty to speak. A person may lie by telling only part of the truth. They may lie by their manner, by insinuations, by inference, or by a shrug of the shoulder.

The weak liar hasn't enough moral stamina to tell the truth when it is disagreeable. Liars of this sort do not want to argue or defend their position. They take the line of least resistance by flattering or lying politely and preferring that a person find out unpleasant truths when they do not have to meet their gaze. I know people who mean to be absolutely honest who can never tell the exact truth when it requires a little moral courage. Cowards are always liars simply because they are too weak to speak the truth.

It takes courage to tell the truth when you know that it may place you in an unfortunate light before the world. It takes courage and character to tell the truth when to do so will be a temporary loss to you. It takes courage and character to tell the truth when it gives a decided advantage to a rival.

The reputation of being beyond price, of being unshaken by any selfish motive and the reputation of always, everywhere, and under all circumstances telling the truth is worth a thousand times more than any temporary gain from deceit.

It does not matter whether you live lies or tell lies, the effect of insincerity upon your character is the same.

Journalists frequently succumb to the temptation of tampering with the truth. They have power to color, distort, misrepresent and over-generalize. They can make a great thing out of a little thing and fail to report events of tragic importance. The reputation of a newspaper is like that of an individual. The newspaper which constantly, knowingly, deceives or sensationalizes stories very soon gets the same kind of reputation as a consummate liar. There are few newspapers in the world which refuse to color the truth, to tamper with facts to suit a favorite theory, party, or person. These few are the solid pillars of journalism. They stand for infinitely more in their community than some other papers with a hundred times more circulation.

One of the most dangerous characters in the business world is the hypocrite who prefers to appear to be on the side of the right but who will quibble or tamper with the truth. The hypocrite is dangerous both as friend and as a foe for they are governed solely by their own self-interest which they believe to be served by appearing to be one thing while in actuality being another. They may not lie outright but leave the truth or part of the truth untold. What such a person gains cannot be compared with what they lose. Liars do not realize that although they may make a little more money by their accomplishments they are diminished as persons every time they misrepresent the truth.

While they add something to their pocket they take something from their integrity.

A great many people believe in the expediency of the policy of lying. They believe that it pays to deceive. Many businesses which are regarded as fairly honest cover up defects in their goods or write misleading advertisements. There are many people who think that deception in business is just about as necessary as money. They believe that it is very difficult, practically impossible, for any person to succeed in a large way and always tell the exact truth about everything.

A superintendent in a large dry goods house once said that he had been busy all the previous day cutting up whole bolts of cloth for remnants. He said that people would willingly pay more for these remnants than they would for yardage from the bolt. How long will the public continue to patronize such a house after it discovers this deception? "Bargains" and "sales" frequently aren't bargains at all. Merchants often sell inferior goods at more than their regular price during sales because they know the deceptive power of suggestion in advertising.

Most of us do not forget favors and kindnesses—or injuries. Once we have been deceived by a business house, a traveling salesman, a solicitor, or a clerk, we do not forget it. That house or clerk loses our business forever.

Even as a working principle honesty is the best policy. Look at the history of business concerns in this country and observe the changes in ownership and identity over the past fifty years. Few of the businesses established fifty years ago are exactly the same today. Some of those which sprang up like mushrooms made a great deal of noise in the business world, did lots of faking and deceptive advertising and flourished for a while. They did not last long. After successfully deceiving their customers for a time they were found out. The failure of a business because of unreliability or dishonesty is very different from the disappearance of a trade name through corporate merging. Not only does it imply immorality in its owners or managers but it hampers the careers of all who worked in the business.

Steady misrepresentation is the most short-sighted policy in the world. No permanent position or institution was every built upon it or ever will be. The person who gets a temporary advantage by misrepresentation makes everybody who finds out about them their enemy ever after. We never fully trust a person or business once we have been deceived. There is no advertisement in the world that can compare with the reputation of being absolutely reliable. This reputation alone has made the names of some businesses in this country worth millions of dollars.

Every time a person deceives they know that they have to cover their tracks. They are always on alert for fear of discovery. The person who is telling the truth and is conscious of their freedom from falsehood has self-assurance in their very act while a liar is always insecure.

No person can be really strong when in the wrong because truth is natural and deception cultivated and abnormal.

Cunning cannot take the place of honesty nor can education. There is always a question mark in our minds when we have dealings with a person who is not absolutely honest. We are not sure of them. On the other hand a person may lack education, culture and even refinement but if they are known to be honest we believe them and we trust them. No person can maintain the appearance of being honest when they are a scoundrel. Their dishonesty shows in their facial expressions and gestures, despite their appearance of respectability with their clothing, and their money. There is a basic lack of self-confidence in the most accomplished and inveterate liar. Sooner or later they betray themselves.

History has been shaped by many persons of charisma who lacked wealth and even position. Charisma can be generated by the narrow and single-minded pursuit of a course of action or by a passionate idealism but it is always generated by persons who believe in their convictions. No modern giant among people generated loyalty through the force of their personality alone. They drew their power from their ability to stand for shared values and from their vigorous pursuit of shared visions.

When a person feels buttressed by principle they do not feel weak although the whole world may be against them. One of the mysteries of the ages has been the marvel of people going to their execution smiling, without a tremor and standing calm and serene while the flames were licking the flesh from their bones. They were supported by a power, not of the flesh, and by the conviction that they were in the right. They believed that they were protected by the Universe and nothing could shake their confidence or disturb their faith. Their exalted mental condition lifted them even above the pain of physical torture.

What do you think of people who attempt to deny the laws of mathematics or act in contradiction to the laws of physics? Even greater fools are those who try to escape justice by lying and deceit. It is true that a person may profit through deception—so may a thief. But deception ultimately is found out. Every so often university students are suspended for cheating in their examinations. A great many otherwise well-intentioned students cheat in all sorts of ways in their examinations. Their methods of cheating are sometimes primitive—they put formulas, figures, suggestions, and all sorts of aids on their shirt cuffs, finger nails, etc. to help them during their examinations. Future forms of deceit and dishonesty on a larger scale may ultimately ruin them.

Many prosperous business people who would never dream of telling verbal lies are consummate liars in the deceits of manufacturing second-rate commodities. I know a man who is always talking to his sons about telling the truth and yet for nearly half a century he has been selling "foreign silks" made in New York or New Jersey.

Liars in high places in American politics have recently had the searchlight of public scrutiny turned upon them. People who not long ago stood high in the regard of the American public are now despised by their fellow business people for their dishonesty. Does it pay to lose one's reputation for a little money?

What use is a fortune gained dishonorably if wherever the owner goes they will be pointed out as a person who has sold out—sold out their honor, their good name, their friends—everything that a person of integrity holds dear?

Chapter 8

Importance of Atmosphere

Domestic and professional tranquility is necessary for one's physical and mental health. The habit of haggling, arguing and quarreling over trifles especially when people are tired erodes your health and character.

Those who quarrel at home when tired after a rough day's work are completely exhausted by the mental irritation and the discord set in motion in their tired brains. Their sleep is troubled and they rise the next morning haggard and worn with no freshness or spontaneity for the new day's work. They feel as though they have been out all night on a drunk.

When will these people learn that harmony is the only condition under which strength of body and beauty of life are perfected? Your best professional work cannot be done in an atmosphere filled with friction. Your home life must be tranquil and restorative as well if you are to be both happy and productive. Sunshine and good cheer and a happy environment bring

out the best in all of us. Our faculties do not work normally
when we are under constant stress. Stress can come from many
sources and haunt our day. Domestic tranquility promotes
strength of purpose, the faculty of concentration and firmness
in action. Liberty—not suffocation, restraint or repression —
creates the atmosphere which develops the best in a person.

Many failures today owe their wretchedness and practical
failure in life to quarreling, faultfinding and habitual bickering.
Irritation and discord are great enemies of health and happiness
while absolute harmony of your character and your environment lead to worthy achievements.

In thousands of homes we see lives which have never
developed to their greatest possibilities and lives which have
never blossomed because of an atmosphere full of discord,
criticism scolding, and constant repression. No one can do
good work when they feel suffocated and oppressed.

Oppression in an office can be just as inhibitive as in the
home. There are business people in executive positions who
have so frequently indulged their short tempers that they are
continually growling at everybody. Finding fault has become
second nature with them. They yield to the first hasty impulse
to scold and make everyone around them uneasy. This constant
growling is a complete failure because employees soon find out
that it is a habit and after a while pay no attention to it. They
are in no way affected by it except that they are embarrassed to
be criticized or scolded in front of others. In the end irritability
in an employer tends to make their employees more careless
and indifferent. A growler does not think of saying kind things
or of praising or encouraging anyone. The employer thinks that
when things go wrong the only way to set them right is to scold
and find fault.

*Why do some of us fuel the fires of irritability when we re-
ally need tranquility?*

Most of the cruelty in the world is thoughtless cruelty. Very
few people intentionally add to their neighbor's load or make

their burden in life heavier or their path rougher. Yet thoughtless thrusts, often flung out in a moment of anger, can wound
badly. We must learn to consider our words before speaking
and especially when we are angry.

Think of how many children have been driven into bad
company by nagging. Frequently you hear of girls who have
run away from home or rushed into an unfortunate marriage or
who keep bad company does so because she was so nagged or
criticized at home that any other place on earth seemed prefer-
able. Young people do not thrive under constant correction and
repression. All healthy young souls crave encouragement and
praise. They will do anything for a father, mother, or teacher
who gives them wise words of appreciation and encouragement
or who urges them to do their best by other means than fault-
finding.

Parents who indulge in habitual nagging often excuse
themselves by saying that it is their love for the boy or girl that
prompts their strictness and criticisms. Their concern is for the
loved one's best interests. Love which displays itself in such a
fashion is apt to remind one of the poetic couplet:

Perhaps it was right to dissemble your love,
But—why did you kick me down stairs?

Nagging instigated by love is love in so unlovely a disguise
that most of its victims agree with the writer who said, "There
is not a bit of love in the nag, however much the nagger may
talk about affection. It is full of unrest and friction and selfishness."

Continual faultfinding, and other negative criticism as well,
is fatal to excellence. Nothing blights the rose more quickly
than a tendency to hunt for flaws and to rejoice in the unlovely
like a hog which always has his nose in the mud and rarely
looks up. Beware of the disposition to see the worst instead of
the best. No matter how many times your confidence has been
betrayed do not allow yourself to sour and do not lose your
faith in people.

Be considerate in your home life. You can make your home a happy place by treating it as special, deserving your greatest tact and charm. There are thousands of people who are polite, tactful and diplomatic toward their customers and business associates but who seem to lock up their good manners in the office at night instead of their cares. These people are mild-mannered Dr.Jekylls in all their business or professional relations but they assume the character of Mr. Hyde as soon as they enter their own homes where they feel at liberty to ride rough-shod over everybody's feelings. They do not seem to think that their mate, or any other member of their family, gets tired or has troubles or their own. After exercising self-restraint all day they go home and vent their bad humor on everybody (even on the dog or cat!). Many people think that home is not a place for self-control. They take it for granted that there they can abuse everybody without restraint there. All this in the place which ought to be the most sacred, most peaceful, and the sweetest.

Instead of thinking of politeness as a repressive exercise and an affair of self-abnegation in self-control try to cultivate an understanding of the positive force of warmth and sensitivity. Courtesy is creative, ingenious, sometimes witty and sometimes divine. Many a thoughtless parent leaves the house in the morning having cast a depressing shadow upon some member of their family. It does not matter to them that their thoughtless words flung out in impatience were received as painfully as if aimed with anger.

Tongue thrusts are infinitely more painful than blows from the hand to many children.

The man or woman whose behavior upon returning home each day is savage and unloving but who can put on a manner as suave and tactful as they employed during the day if company is present, is hypocritical. This sort of person grunts and growls as soon as their guests leave, snarls at their mate, nags and finds fault with the children and because their reputation is no longer at stake feels free to relieve themself of all their pent up frustrations and angers.

In this climate of nervous irritability the better-bred person is always placed at a disadvantage. The finer the character and more sensitive the nature the more the victim who possesses them is handicapped. Disadvantaged by his or her own sense of what is right they may feel disgust or resentment but have a difficult time expressing these feelings. Either the mate submits to tyranny or tension in the home mounts and tempers explode, and the family disintegrates. One cannot be civilized some of the time and a bear the rest of the time without slips in one's behavior.

What we do habitually we do naturally.

Company manners can be dangerous—they are like formal clothes that are worn only occasionally. The wearer never becomes sufficiently used to them to become comfortable or feel easy and is always betraying the fact. Like style in dress which must be habitual enough for the wearer not to feel selfconscious about it, good manners must become so essential a part of one's life that we practice them spontaneously and unconsciously.

Not long ago I visited a home where such exceptionally good breeding prevailed and such politeness was exhibited by all the members of the family toward one another that it made a great impression upon me.

This home is a school for good manners. The children are brought up so accustomed to polite behavior that they do not know what "company manners" means. The boys have been taught to treat their sisters with as much deference as they would show to guests. The politeness, courtesy, and consideration with which the members of this family treat one another are most refreshing and beautiful. Coarseness, gruffness, and a lack of delicacy find no place there. Both boys and girls have been trained from infancy to be pleasant and to try to make others happy. The entire family makes it a rule to dress before dinner in the evening just as others would if company were expected. In this manner they show the special regard they have for one another. At table everyone expects to be at his best and they leave their grouches and worries behind. There is a sort of rivalry to see who can be the most entertaining or contribute the most playful bits of conversation. There are no indication of indigestion in this family because everyone is trained to laugh and do their best to make the meal a really happy occasion. Laughter is the enemy of indigestion, as this family proves.

The etiquette of the table is also strictly observed as a act of kindness which is practiced for the joy of it not for the sake of creating a good impression on friends or acquaintances. There is in this home an air of peculiar refinement which is very charming. The children are taught early to greet callers and guests cordially and in a hearty and hospital fashion and to make them feel very welcome. They are taught to make everyone relaxed and at ease. As a result of their training, the children in this family have formed a habit of good behavior and are considered a blessing to any gathering. They are not embarrassed by the awkward slips and inconsistencies which are so mortifying to those who only wear their company manners on special occasions.

Many parents seem to expect their children to pick up their good manners outside the home in school or while visiting. This is a fatal mistake. Every home should be a school of good manners and good breeding. The children should be taught that there is nothing more important than the development of an interesting personality, an attractive presence, and an ability to entertain with grace and ease. They should be taught that the great object of life is to develop a noble manhood or womanhood, even in this vulgar age and that an attractive personality can contribute to their ease in life. There is no art like that of beautiful behavior and no wealth greater than that of a pleasing personality and gracious manner.

Some might argue that today politeness is quaint and hardly a necessity for success but this is not the case. Many a business executive is deferential to their superiors in position or wealth but is shoddy in their treatment of their employees. If they could be as alert to the needs of his secretaries or employees as they are to the wishes of those they seek to impress, they would find them more responsive to their needs. Authority, efficiency, and productivity are all greatly improved by consideration and tact. An employer who rides roughshod over the sensitive feelings of those who take orders from them with domineering acts, criticizing, mercilessly scolding, and using obscene and profane language, demeans themselves in such treatment.

People are, to a certain extent, judged by their quality even in the market-place. Do not under-rate a person merely because they work for a small salary. They may be infinitely finer-grained than their employer. By the same token, you should not over-estimate the acquaintance of a coarse cruel person who pays not the slightest heed to his employees' feelings.

Above all you must become aware of your importance to others. No life remains the same after you have once touched it. You have the power to encourage hope or despair in others. Will you by thoughtless cruelty and deepen the shadow which hangs over a life or will you by kindness dispel it altogether? No matter how you feel personally, no matter what is disturbing your peace of mind, do not allow yourself to utter a cruel or unkind word or thought. The faultfinder, the sarcastic person, the person who is always giving someone a thrust in the back, does an immense amount of harm in a community. People who throw gloomy shadows wherever they go, who depress everybody, and who see only their own opportunity make bad company, bad work companions bad mates. As a rule they are unsuccessful, unpopular and little mourned when they die.

Emulate the person who cheers, inspires and encourages others. You want the person who always has a kind word ready and who is ever anxious to give their hand and their help. Such a person is loved during life and missed after death.

Those who are thinking of marrying should find out how

their prospective mate acts in business. If the person you are interested in is not considerate to those who they employ then they will probably make a brute of a mate. In the intimacy of married life the wear and tear of business sometimes brings out the worst in a person.

How much of a liar are you willing to put up with?

Chapter 9

The Joy of Giving

There is a story told of a great king whose only son was the sole object of his devotion. The boy had everything he desired and all that wealth and love could provide but he was not happy. His sad face, his scowls of discontent, made his father miserable. The king promised great wealth to anyone who could release his child from the power of gloom. A greatly renowned magician showed up at the palace one day promising that he could turn the prince's scowls to smiles and his sorrow to joy. "If you can do this", said the king, "I will give you whatever you ask." The old magician took the boy to a palace chamber that was set up with the apparatus of an alchemist. With great show he distilled a clear liquid which he poured into an ink-well. Taking a great ostrich feather quill he wrote on parchment with the precious liquid. Then, handing the parchment to the boy, the magician explained that the rest of the cure now lay in the boy's own hands. The magician was to depart and the boy himself to bring out the secret writing by means of a flame held under the parchment in a darkened room. The boy was then to follow the instructions explicitly.

Impressed, the young prince did as he was told. When the boy lit the flame he found a simple message in a beautiful blue scrawl: "Relieve the suffering of at least one of your father's subjects every day the rest of your life." It was in feeding the poor, caring for the ill, clothing and housing the homeless, that the young prince was relieved of the torments of gloom. Success cannot be measured in material terms.

Unless you are somewhat happy you cannot pride yourself in your achievements. A gladness born in others happiness and an unselfish good will can enlarge the scope of our lives. When we improve the lives of those around us in free acts of generosity we gain an intangible blessing which nurtures our own growth. The more we radiate encouragement and hope, the more they come back to us.

Like the sun which lights our world yet never seems to lose anything or to grow smaller, the more we give the more we have.

Yet there is a strange weakness of human nature which blinds many of us to the good in others. We delight in careless unkindness and hurting people instead of helping them. The habitual belittler who never sees any good in anything which does not immediately concern them and advance their interests. The insincere person who is always sticking a knife into other people's backs and making light of other people's motives or finding defects in their characters. These are the types of character which exhibit pettiness of soul.

It is painful to a small person to hear a competitor complimented. They always try to diminish the praise of another by a malicious "if" or "but" or to cast doubt upon the character of the person praised.

The habit of belittling is a confession of weakness. It betrays a small, jealous, envious nature and, usually, a life that is not well poised and balanced. The magnanimous personality has no room for jealousy or a belittling spirit. Do not exhibit your own narrowness of soul by maintaining silence when you should praise someone or by billeting a competitor. In disparaging others, in discounting the achievements of competitors, one exposes the limitations of his own personality.

We *do not understand that when we draw a picture of others we also draw one of ourselves.*

Unfortunately people of great ability who have been distinguished for brilliant intellectual gifts, unusual courage, or tenacity of purpose frequently have been insanely jealous and envious of others, especially those in the same profession or business as themselves. Success does not imply greatness. A person with a really large nature is generous and charitable even to his worst enemy.

All sorts of people—singers and actors and, I am sorry to say, some ministers—suffer from professional jealousy. This insecurity seems to be more characteristic of people in the professions than of those in business.

I know a minister who would be very popular and successful if he could see the good in his fellow ministers but he cannot. He is always emphasizing their faults and weaknesses, especially if they are becoming popular. When anyone praises another minister. He will say, "Yes, he is a pretty good man, but he is not always absolutely reliable in his statements", or "He is very free in his use of other preachers' sermons; he is a great borrower of ideas." He seldom has a good thing to say about other ministers.

One reason why some professional people get such paltry results from their work in life is that they do not understand that all professions are vocational and that they involve the commitment of one's total personality. One can bracket a job in a businesslike fashion to a set number of hours in a day but one can never bracket one's ethical and emotional commitment to one's profession. By treating their professions as mere jobs some of today's doctors, lawyers, teachers, and priests have weakened society and diminished their own mystique. Professional jealousy frequently stems from a sense of your lack of total commitment to your profession.

It is astonishing how rapidly a person develops when they dedicate their life to the service of others. There is nothing so beneficial in life as the early formation of character in service for others. Good will, like honesty, is self-rewarding.

A philosopher once asked his pupils, "What is the most desirable good in the world?" After many answers had been given, someone finally said, "a good heart." ."True," said the philosopher, "You have expressed in three words what all that the rest have said. One that has a good heart will be content, a good companion and neighbor and will easily find their proper course of action in life."

A good heart may hide under a rough exterior but is most manifest in a kindly disposition and a frank cordial manner. These are riches beside which the fortune of a miserly multi-millionaire diminishes in importance. With these traits a person can do as much good as the most generous philanthropist. We cannot help admiring and loving persons of a open and generous nature. Whole communities are often cheered by one of these radiant personalities. What a blessing it is to meet a cheery manner and a sunny disposition. What a gift it is to be able to lighten the burdens upon the shoulders of those around us.

Many of us are so blinded by our zeal for personal gain that we do not judge the value and importance of people and situations. We take our criteria for behavior from the market-place little realizing that it is we who must shape the world and not the other way around. When we analyze the features of our fellow-workers' personalities it should be with an eye for making the most of their good points. Only in this way can we hope to bring out the best in them and make the most of our relations with them.

Stories abound concerning the good that has been wrought by a kind word at the right time. A woman once invited a ragged dirty beggar into her home, fed him a comfortable meal, gave him clean clothes and sent him on his way after telling him that he was made for something better than tramping. It was a shame, she said, for a man of his apparent intelligence and good health to be getting a living in such a disgraceful way. Years afterward when she had forgotten all about the tramp she had befriended a well-groomed businessman knocked on her door. The man explained that he was the tramp whom she had once taken into her home and treated like a brother. Her kindness on that occasion had been a turning point for him and made a man of him again. He had since prospered beyond his deserts, he said, and ever since he had gotten on his feet he had wanted to express his gratitude to his benefactress.

From the way many of us push and trample one another in our mad rush for money one would think that we felt no ties of humanity binding us together. Everywhere we see people in distress whom we could help and do not. We excuse ourselves by saying it is none of our business. Yet we can enlarge the dignity of our fellow, as well as ourselves, by high expectations and kindness.

Here is another example from that extraordinary group of mortals, the tramps, where the tramp out-did his benefactress. A tramp was begging for food from house to house in the fall, and knocked on the door of a woman who provided him with something to eat. "Here", she said, "eat this, and if you want to show your gratitude, just happen around here some morning after a snow-storm and clean off our sidewalk."

The woman awakened one winter morning to the sound of scraping outside the house. The tramp to whom she had given food was clearing her sidewalk of a heavy fall of snow. When he caught sight of his benefactress at the window he raised his tattered hat to her and his self-imposed task finished went away without saying a word or even asking for anything to eat. Three times during the winter the man returned and repeated the chore never once asking for compensation or food.

Cultivate an open nature, a kindly manner, and a generous spirit. The persistent effort to radiate sunshine, cheer, hope and good will not only brings light and joy to other hearts but opens wide the door to your own happiness. If you cannot give material help, if you have no money to give, you can always help others by cordial words of sympathy, kindness and encouragement. There are more hearts hungering for love and sympathy than for money and to these you can always help.

Consider the poignancy of the remark of the poor foreigner who responded to a kind-hearted offer of assistance by saying that he was "Looking for conversation". If the English was broken the sentiment was, nevertheless, vividly expressed. Loneliness is as devastating as the need for material necessities. We all like the person who flings the door of their heart wide open and bids us welcome. One who sees a brother in every person they meet instead of a rival, competitor, or possible enemy. The kindly disposed person has an infinite advantage over someone whose withdrawn selfishness repels people instead of attracting them. Do not withdraw from new acquaintances and shut up like a clam and dare to give your best to everyone you meet.

The true cultivation of personality and character is possible only when one has a generous vision of one's fellows. Personal growth, civic enterprise and world progress depend upon it. Generosity is apparent in a frank cordial manner—a manner that is perfectly transparent and that conceals no guile, covers no malice. Generosity is the source of personal warmth. Whether for good or for ill, much of one's success depends upon one's personality. There is nothing so unattractive as an icy, formal, suspicious manner.

I have sat at restaurant tables where hostile table companions have made it positively depressing to eat there. One's bad manner can forbid not only conversation but any friendly gesture. On the other hand, I have sat at a table with foreigners who could not speak a word of English but whose cordial, gracious salute as I sat down warmed me for the rest of the day. Their manner spoke a language all nationalities understand. It was the language of good will. Habitual good will has a powerful influence on others. It lifts all minds above petty jealousies and meannesses and it enriches and enlarges one's whole experience. If you possess a spirit of good will, even if you are shy, you will be able to feel a certain kinship with and friendliness toward all, even towards complete strangers. Do not be afraid to radiate friendliness and others will radiate it back to you.

Some time ago while travelling in the Southwest in the hottest weather I noticed a young man on the train who seemed to get acquainted with his fellow passengers without effort. He made the otherwise dreary trip a real pleasure because of his good spirits. His face was so radiant and he seemed so animated by a healthy good nature that it did one good to look at him. He was eager to help everyone and to tell all that he knew about the country through which we were passing. It is easy to believe that his cheerfulness and cordial manner have won him universal welcome and greatly aided his career.

The chords struck by some people are all in a minor key. They sound a note of pessimism everywhere. Their outlook is gloomy and times are always hard and money tight. Everything in them seems to be contracting. Nothing in their lives leads to the expansion or growth of their personalities.

With others the opposite seems to be true. They radiate sunshine. Every bud they touch opens its petals and exudes its fragrance. By some happy alchemy they are able to perceive and bring out the best in people.

Life is short. What a satisfaction it is to feel that we have scattered joy instead of woe in people's lives! Whether you succeed or fail in your occupation if you have succeeded in encouraging others, in inspiring them and cheering them on, your life will have joy. It is infinitely better to fail in business and to succeed in this, your vocation as a person, than to accumulate vast wealth but be unable to help others.

The greatest monuments are not in marble or in bronze but in human hearts. The monuments are built to the unselfish and to those who, whatever else their calling, are fulfilling their most general but most emphatic call—that of being human.

Chapter 10

Power and the Self

Within every human being there is energy which if given proper direction can bring to fruition the most ambitious ideals. There are no sealed orders within the brain and heart unaccompanied by the ability to execute them. The ability to achieve and to actualize our dreams lies within us.

If the desire to be free is written in your blood, if it is part of the very texture of your being, you will have within you the strength to break whatever binds you and holds you back.

Freedom from the shackles of our environment is accomplished by not by running away but by overcoming the obstacles near at hand. Our longing will not be magically satisfied on some far-off mountain or in some distant and exotic locale with just a wish. For most of us, the ideal that haunts our soul to excel must be realized within the sphere of the familiar. In average cities and in towns, in the workshop and in the office.

In short, within the circumscribed limits of our daily duties is the field where we must accomplish our ideal.

The strength to achieve in spite of obstacles can only be developed with persistence and determination. All our reserves must be utilized and all our powers concentrated and wisely directed toward our goals if we are to accomplish the work we have marked out for ourselves. We cannot scatter our attention on a thousand things at once.

When the particular work we do appears to contribute nothing to our ultimate goals we should regard it as an opportunity for developing necessary skills and habits. We must always be ready to seize with daring all opportunities that come our way to realize our goals. We must also cultivate the time-honored virtues of perseverance and patience which more than genius itself can effect change.

As we proceed in life we may find our ideals changing and deepening. Everywhere we see people starving for love and dying for appreciation and concern. Men and women who possess material comfort and who are able to gratify almost every wish can still be hungry for affection. Much of what goes by the name of universal love is only selfishness. Until love extends beyond the narrow circle of relatives and friends and beyond the boundaries or one's own interests and needs it is not real love.

There is no doubt that those who are filled with a spirit of love—whose sympathies and tenderness are not confined to their immediate relatives and friends, but reach out to every member of the human family— live more fully than those who are selfish and pessimistic. Do not believe there is any human being, in prison or out, so depraved that nobody could influence them by love, kindness and patience.

I have known men and women who had such charm of manner and such great, loving hearts that the most hardened characters responded to their influence. Such people could never have been reformed by punishment or compulsion. Love was the only power that could have reached them.

There was a man who had served, at different times, twenty-five years in prisons. No sooner would he get out of prison than he would begin to plan some burglary which would send him back again. The police all knew him. A great many people tried to help him but every time he got a position he lost it because someone who knew him circulated the report that he was an ex-convict.

He happened to fall under the influence of a great woman who did not ask him about his past. She did not want to have anything to do with the criminal but only with the person. She told him that he had a keen brain and that success and happiness were his birthright and that all he had to do was claim them. He had no right to look upon himself as a debased creature but should always strive to live up to his good qualities. She urged him not to go skulking about the streets or to regard himself as a criminal that is hunted by the police and detectives but to say to himself words of encouragement.

The man faithfully followed her advice, repeating to himself the words she had given him, reminding himself of his dignity and possibilities. After a while he became so transformed that the very lines of discouragement in his face disappeared. The uplifting self-image given him by his friend awakened a sense of his essential humanity and appealed to the best in him. By evoking the qualities which had been buried all those years, a woman completely changed a man's life.

Forget yourself. You will never do anything great until you do. Self-consciousness is a disease for many. No matter what they do they cannot get away from their self-preoccupation. They become wrapped up in self-analysis, wondering how they look, what others think of them, and how they can best serve their own interests. Even less petty introspection can be unhealthy. When every thought and every effort seems to focus upon self nothing radiates outward and nothing returns to refresh the root's of one's being. Self-consciousness halts the expansion of the personality and kills aspiration and cripples executive ability.

The mind which accomplishes things worth while looks out, not in and it is focussed upon its objects not upon itself.

Perhaps the greatest prayers have been the silent longings and the secret yearnings of the heart. It is important to see these longings rewarded by actualities. Yet the real test of a person's success is their daily life. Do they really live?

Are their best qualities hidden and unexpressed in action? What does it matter how much money one has if only a small part of the real person is alive and if they have no sympathies and if their appreciation of the beautiful and their love of the good have dissipated.

In our personal development most of us are at least slightly lop-sided and some of us are monstrosities. Frequently one faculty is enormously over-developed at the expense of all the others. The effect is similar to that of a tree which has all but one branch lopped off and that branch has a large and undisciplined growth. How rare it is to find a fully poised person, one who is perfectly balanced.

The best legacy that a person can leave their children is the memory and influence of a broad finely developed mentality, a well-disciplined mind and a magnanimous spirit. Let your children remember that you brought them up to respect themselves and to have an ethical sense, to be self-reliant, strong, vigorous and independent and to do their own thinking so that they could become leaders instead of tag-alongs. They will be confident that there is power within them to help them live their own lives rather than to depend upon the success or failure of others. How many people in this country are ashamed of their parents—the parents whose money they are spending! They are glad enough to get the money but they know full well the lack in their parent's characters and the poverty of their lives.

Isn't it sad how people will struggle and strive in order to pile up money for their children and at the same time sell their own lives, their very life-blood, into dollars often leaving no memory which can be revered? Is it not strange that parents will contend so fiercely for that which is shallow and neglect the development of more permanent goods? Surely these otherwise shrewd parents ought to be able to see that the chances are small that their children will develop the power and self-reliance necessary for a satisfying life when everyone is telling them that they are fools to work and that their fathers are rich and that they should just have a good time.

The chances of developing the qualities which form character in the child are increased not by amassing a fortune to corrupt its inheritors but by instilling a love for what is priceless in human life: integrity, loyalty and friendship. If a person is too great to be measured in dollars or defined by property; if the wealth of one's personality has overflowed until all one's neighbors feel richer for one's acquaintance; if every foot of land in your community is worth more because you live there, then no loss of property can destroy you.

It is sometimes difficult to be philosophical about material loss. But we all know people whose influence far exceeds their material wealth. It gives a sense of immense satisfaction to think that there is something greater than our wealth or business and something which will survive robbery and persecution. If we possess it, it will even outlast the body itself.

Something within us protests against the idea that our most precious possessions can be at the mercy of accident or uncertainty. The feeling of serenity and the assurance of stability and of possessing that which no power can shake arises out of a vision of ones place in the universe. Not all stable personalities are wonderful persons! But if one's serenity arises from a sense of one's role in a moral rather than mechanistic universe and if one believes that each form of existence brings from the unseen its own lesson of wisdom, power, and design you will never crumble before your private losses.

The true life of the self is beyond destruction.

Chapter 11

The Guarantee of Success

The person who can think clearly and act wisely is sought for important positions for obvious reasons. Everybody likes to feel that they will be safe in an emergency. It is the person who knows what to do when others are disconcerted and who is cool when others are flustered that will be asked to handle the pressure of decision-making. Not everyone likes to assume great responsibility and not everyone should. But surely there is something admirable in a person who has the wisdom and judgment to assess situations and act quickly when necessary.

It is a difficult thing to remain level-headed in all circumstances and under all conditions. It shows a reserve power that is characteristic of the truly poised self-controlled person. But there is more to decision making power than a cool head.

Consider the analogy of serenity and poise under all conditions to the iceberg at sea. No matter how the weather rages or how the waves dash against its sides, it does not tremble or quiver or give any signs of instability because 7/8 of its enormous bulk is below the surface of the water. Its immensity is securely balanced down in the calm of the ocean depths beneath the agitation of the sea. It is this tremendous reserve below the surface which makes the exposed part of the iceberg bid defiance to the elements.

Many people, like the iceberg, have great stability but that does not mean it can think correctly. It is not enough merely to maintain equilibrium. One must make decisions, often quickly, on the basis of an accurate assessment of situations. One cannot merely flow with the current popular opinion when in a position of authority.

Here is another basic characteristic of executive ability: ambition thrives in adversity. Somehow, ease comfort and the thought of prosperity take the spring out of ambition. The motive to push ahead, the impulse to struggle and strive, is sometimes weakened by the feeling that you have already achieved your goal and that you have gained what you started out to get. It is proper to reward ourselves with a feeling of self-satisfaction when we have attained our goals, but we must deepen and extend our ambitions after we have satisfied our immediate needs.

We must become ambitious for the welfare of others as well as ourselves.

If you want a sense of fulfillment in life there is one thing you ought always to be able to do no matter what your circumstances. You must be able to keep calm and act deliberately when others are confused and excited in order to have a leading part to play in life. You will have tremendous power in the community and be sought out in great emergencies and you will be looked for in crisis. The shaky person, the waverer, the person who is never certain of himself cannot expect to have authority. With rare exceptions only through authority can a person make significant changes or contributions to the community.

Emotional balance itself is not, however, merely the result of the proper proportion of daring and judgment. We all know the development of the personality in the give-and-take of human experience is necessary to produce confidence in decision-making. It is true that only persons of strong character are given positions of authority or are trusted in times of crisis but sometimes these do not come to the fore because they lack personal charm and thus feel insecure. The development of the personality takes place in the same situations where character is formed. Thus education and personal charm are complementary assets to a well-formed character.

In a perfectly adjusted machine every part is made with reference to every other part. The movement of every wheel in a perfect timepiece must be exquisitely adjusted to the entire watch and each wheel be suited to every other wheel in the watch. Personal charm is one of the wheels of the human watch. It is no more or less important than another part. You would not boast of your watch because it has a very powerful mainspring. Likewise, you would not boast of a nice personality. We value a watch for its ability to keep time for this is its purpose.

We value a human for their ability to help others, for that is their purpose.

However lovable a person may be if they do not exhibit a strong sense of their role in the complex machine of contemporary society they appear weak. Today many people are asked to assume a variety of roles in life and sometimes these rules conflict. The criteria for choosing among several positions must not be simply monetary. Besides the personal value you attach to the work itself you should consider its value or worth for the world. Many positions prevent one from exercising authority. Let yourself be driven by an ambition worthy of a full person. Have the ambition of shaping your world for the better even if it is only in a small or local way.

The "enlightenment" of ambition is in part accomplished by education whether in the class room or self taught. Education today is not generally conceived to produce well-rounded individuals.

If they are truly to understand the ethical problems of the age, young men and women must seek to complement their training for life with either more acquaintance with the humanities or with more introduction to science and technology.

Formal education today has become training for occupations and professions. The fact that it often fails to land people jobs is frequently due to the fact that the education;is not well informed in a marketplace that changes rapidly. Furthermore, certain qualities required by all executive positions are not implanted in the classroom.

The training and education of today's youth is not calculated to develop true intellectual maturity. Unfortunately, many employed in the academic machine fail to see the use of such a quality. In many technical schools a discipline or science is well-taught in its specifics and this is usually at the loss or expense of "total education." There is simply not time for both.

Consequently, especially before the college level, students should be introduced to all that is exciting in the intellectual world today. The great object of early training should be to exercise all the powers of observation and intellect and to promote the balance of physical and mental training. For those who have not reached maturity one sided development and forced special training are the great curses of modern life. Although they may have job security early, over-specialization and a lack of a universal balanced program of general education can cause serious problems both for them in middle life and for those with whom they work. When such persons are put in positions of authority they often cannot grasp fully the ethical problems that confront them. They frequently lack vocational commitment (they do not comprehend what it is). On the level of decision-making they are well-trained in certain areas but lack the sub-surface strength of the iceberg so praised above. They have no intellectual reservoirs, they have no elasticity of intellect and hence no ingenuity. They are educationally deprived and they may be difficult to convince of their lacks.

One-sided minds, no matter how brilliant in some particular faculty, are no more balanced, than the tree whose sap has been directed to one lone branch after its other members have been lopped off. True mental poise is the result of mental harmony. When life hangs in the balance the poised physician or surgeon always has the advantage over one who is full of fear and loses his head. At a great trial it is the lawyer who maintains his equanimity who often carries weight with the jury simply because he is capable of greater lucidity and responsiveness than is the sincere ranter.

Mental poise enables us to consider the possibilities of the future, both our own and those of mankind as a whole. In an age when one can travel around the world in less than a week's time there is still poverty disease and hunger, both physical and spiritual. Many people who consider their lives satisfactory are content to be half persons rather than to dare to seek the improvement of their world. A comfortable world of "good vibrations" for the chosen— is this the best possible world? A life of ease, a life of pleasant security— is this all we want when we know that others are suffering? There are all kinds of ways of "improving the universe." In countless small ways we can improve our own community and extend the community feeling.

There is a tremendous amount of force in a single atom yet this force is silent and all but invisible. The harmony of Nature is the result of an intricate set of often hidden relationships and the strength of Nature is often quiet. The water in a little mountain brook dashing down over the rocks makes more noise than the mighty Mississippi River when it flows between peaceful banks.

Weak characters, like empty wagons, are noisy. They fuss

and fume and accomplish little.

The effectiveness of our labor depends upon all our faculties working together in harmony. We often see a person without any apparent talent or brilliant faculties succeed where others of seemingly greater capacities fail. It is because the leader's roles are not in conflict with one another— they have what the psychologists call a "fully integrated personality." Our personalities roles and powers are so interrelated that the improvement of any one faculty of the mind, like the improvement of the judgment, strengthens all its other capacities. A child does not realize the problems they will have later in life if they do not form the habit of sawing the wood straight or of driving the nail true, or of finishing any project completely. This defect will not only hamper their career but it will demoralize them, weaken their judgment, affect their industry and ambition, and in general lower their expectations in life.

A child is more likely to develop into a successful contributive member of a community if they begin early in life to make decisions. The child brought up in a rural area has different advantages from those of the city-bred youth. In general, the city youth can be said to experience the benefits rather than hardships of independence. For the city youth, ingenuity and creativity will find their outlets anywhere but rural children have more opportunities to learn to use tools with skill and to bring into existence projects about which city children can only dream. Rural life ought to offer a child more opportunities for beneficial contact with Nature though it often seems to do just the opposite - breeding indifference to what is always present. A city child can find exquisite beauty in a clump of weeds growing in a gutter and sometimes does.

It is less injurious to be poor in rural areas than in the city. Yet in any setting the child whose parents can foster education and growth, provide cultural roots, and inspire the child to worthwhile goals, is richer by far than the child whose nurture is impersonal and sterile.

Versatile level-headed people are scarce. They are always at a premium. We frequently find competent people doing strange unbusinesslike things. The reputation of being erratic or a little bit off in your judgment or of doing foolish things so that people cannot rely upon you is fatal to advancement. Versatility that is not erratic. Competency that is characterized by daring and ingenuity are the gifts of a good upbringing and education. You can make them yours by continually striving for knowledge and discipline.

Prudence, too, is essential. Our country is full of disappointed lives in which victories have been swallowed up by defeat. Effective strokes marred by unfortunate slips because a great ambition was hampered by a total lack of system and an inability to learn from the result of great efforts.

Employees are often surprised at the advancement to a responsible position of one of their number who is less brilliant than many others. Their employer is not looking for brilliance but for good sense, soundness of judgment and levelheadedness. In his search for a level-headed practical person, an employer often passes by the college graduate, the careful and precise person, and even the genius. The employer knows that the stability of his business depends upon employees with good judgment and common sense. These are the mainstay of their establishment.

Most young people do not realize how much their success depends upon their general reputation for honesty and "square dealing," and for good sound judgment. It will make all the difference in the world to you to see what people think of you and how they estimate your abilities. Those who are in a position to help you financially are always looking for hard business sense. If you lack that, or the appearance of it, you may have trouble securing financial backing even if you are known to be a person of otherwise excellent qualities.

Confidence and self-assurance in prospective employees are among the chief considerations of employers. We have heard bankers and people at the head of all sorts of business concerns ask the same questions about an applicant for an important position, "Is she a person upon whom you can rely?" "Does he have determination, stamina, staying qualities?" "Can you depend upon him in an emergency?" "Is she stable?" The assessment of these qualities is largely based upon one's ability to present oneself in a self-assured and confident manner. Personal poise greatly aids one's chances in business and enables one to show off the best qualities of character. The person who exposes to view their worries over trifles reveals a certain lack of self-control. They show that they have not discovered themselves and do not know their innate power. They have not claimed their birthright of inner harmony. They reveal that they have not discovered how they can be prosperous and happy. They have conquered only a little corner of themselves.

We take it for granted that a person who cannot control them self cannot control others and that they are not suited for leadership. Self-assurance comes, in part, from the conviction that one has the qualities of common sense and sound judgment in decision-making. This conviction arises in the exercise of one's faculties in real-life situations.

One reason why the majority of people have such poor judgment is that they do not depend upon it. Unused faculties develop no more than do unused muscles. Many people rely on conventional behavior to pull them through every situation. The habitual exercise of one's judgment in every situation, no matter how trifling, will multiply efficiency a thousand-fold.

You can get along without a great many things in the world if necessary, including a post-degree education but you cannot get on in the world without good judgment. Multitudes of graduates are turned out every year with a large amount of theoretical knowledge who have not had a particle of training or experience in their chosen fields. Although academic policies are rapidly changing and many college and university departments offer academic credit for field-work like practice teaching, etc., there is still a wide gap between theoretical disciplines and professional job markets.

We often hear people say that they cannot understand why someone has had such a mediocre career or has been a failure when he or she had such a brilliant start at school. At the same time it is the rarest thing in the world for a person with good judgment to fail even if he or she is not brilliant. Though they may make occasional mistakes the person of sound judgment will always get on his feet again. The person who has brilliant strokes now and then but who is freakish in their decisions because they are the victim of poor judgment may be hired but will not win positions of authority.

If you want the reputation of being a level-headed person you must act like one. Most people find themselves almost constantly occupied in petty affairs when they would like to be doing other things. Not only does this make them unhappy but it lessens the probability of their acquiring and exercising the faculty of good judgment.

When we feel strongly impelled to follow a certain course of action or to do something in a certain way but we do not do so we may live to regret our past decisions, worry over them and lack confidence in the future.

On the other hand, if we form a habit of "thinking things through," of evaluating each situation in decision-making and if we make it a policy to do what we believe we should do, when we should do it and in the way we honestly think is best and if we never allow ourselves to shrink responsibility because it interferes with our comfort or leisure, then we shall become truly remarkable for the excellence of our lives.

We constantly hear people say, "I know that I ought to do this thing today, but I don't think I'm going to get to it," or "I don't feel like it." If we find that we tend to procrastinate or let things slide, if we find ourselves doing just the opposite of what we know we ought to do then we should ask ourselves why. Those who expect to make the most of themselves must take themselves in hand just as they would a pupil or child and no matter how disagreeable or difficult the task they need to discipline themselves to do what is necessary. Opting for the easiest course of action is not always the best decision.

A very successful man who found that he was getting into the habit of letting things slide along and doing the easier task first and putting off the difficult chore, suddenly realized that if the habit became fixed it would seriously handicap his career. He turned completely around and forced himself to begin his work early in the morning. He first tackled what he felt he ought to do in the way that appealed to his best judgment without regard for his feelings, leisure or comfort. The result was that within a very short time he had developed a strong vigorous character and now finds it comparatively easy to do what he must do each day. He himself says that unless he had taken himself in hand and trained himself as would a teacher his pupil, forcing himself to do whatever was wisest at a given time, he would have wrecked his career because he was naturally inclined to take things easy. Great characters have felt the necessity of stern self-discipline.

Force yourself to do what you know you ought to do instead of consulting your comfort or convenience. You will very materially strengthen your character and your judgment and you will also increase your reputation for levelheadedness. Working in a disciplined fashion does not mean pushing yourself through tedious tasks that you detest— remember you must always be ready to seize the opportunity to accomplish what you have chosen as your goal or goals. Nor does discipline entail over-work. We have seen that the person who is the continual grind, who never takes a vacation and never sets apart time for relaxing in his day or week becomes more and more irritable and ceases to provide for their own happiness.

Discipline allows us to vault easily over the hurdles of the day. Deplore it as we will, most of us are lazy and we like to get out of as much disagreeable work as possible. We do not like to do things that interfere with our comfort or which tax and perplex us. Because we have taken the easy road so often most of us have fallen into the habit of avoiding the difficult, shunning the disagreeable and of procrastinating by putting off uncomfortable tasks until they become more and more distasteful. Procrastination is a sign that we do not think that we can do exactly the right thing. Again, it is an exhibition of a lack of self-confidence or self-control.

The way to avoid the sting of a nettle is to grasp it vigorously quickly. The way to take the discomfort out of a disagreeable task is to do it quickly and vigorously. Rather than playing with your work and torturing yourself over what you dislike about it, attack every project with determination and see it through to completion.

Daring is indispensable for great success but if it is not balanced by a certain shrewdness and prudence it can lead us into all sorts of fool-hardy ventures. Boldness is a great quality when it is unleashed by caution and good judgment. I know a woman who is deficient in caution in her business. She does not know what fear means and she plunges into all sorts of foolish projects which do not turn out well. Consequently, she is always trying to get out of things into which she has plunged too hastily. If her prudence had been matched by her boldness she would have made a very successful businesswoman.

Whatever your beliefs do not get morbid or cranky about any subject for it is inevitably fatal to advancement. Some of the ablest young men and women I know have been fearfully handicapped in their efforts to get on because they have developed into irritable persons.

Many people persist in airing their personal beliefs, current fads and eccentric tastes at every opportunity. They regard this as their sacred duty and feel that it would be cowardly not to declare themselves on all sorts of issues. They find the opportunity of airing their beliefs and theories irresistible.

People only reward the results of outspokenness if it is

natural. The fact is that people are afraid of zealots or even the merely over-enthusiastic. Extreme behavior indicates a lack of balance to many people. They are prejudiced against all peculiarities because conventions rather than conviction are the standards of behavior for them. Even if your goal in life is to see those standards raised and imbued with greater ideal-ism you must be realistic about the world of your day-to-day existence.

In other words, employers are in general afraid of people with lop-sided personalities. They are also afraid of personal peculiarities that indicate departures from the normal. I recall a man of good qualities who is a food-faddist. He is one of the most intelligent men I know but you cannot talk to him five minutes without his trying to draw you into a discussion of food values and to convince you that the real reason you are fat or thin, have indigestion, poor sight, rheumatism, etc. is because of the constituents of your diet or that you suffer from eating over-processed food and drink. He will proceed to go into the chemistry of foods and the physiology of digestive processes until you get disgusted and leave him and you are intending to keep out of his way in the future.

Another acquaintance of mine, a man of great ability, has become crazy about medicine. Every time you see him he has some new remedy which he believes will benefit eveyone's physical condition if only people would just try it. He nearly ruined his own health in his experiments and although he has a healthy body he has lost clout in his community because of his reputation as a crank.

People who get carried away with fads and excesses, or who become preoccupied with any one problem usually very susceptible to suggestion. Any new fad that is epidemic they catch. Crash diets, easy formulas for curing shyness, have a regular run with them and they are carried away until some-thing new comes along.

Self-preoccupied people are narrow. They lack breadth,

sympathy and generosity. The magnanimous and charitable soul does not think they are right and everybody else is wrong. They give everybody a fair chance. They are charitable and broad and generous towards those who differ with them because they know that they are just as liable to be mistaken as others.

There was once a wealthy man who refused to pay for a yacht built for him by a boat-builder with a great name because it had too much sail for the ballast. The issue went to court. The skipper of the boat testified at the trial that he did not dare put out all the sail except in moderate weather because of the danger of capsizing. The boat was all right in pleasant weather but dangerous in a storm.

There are plenty of people like that boat. They have too much sail and too little ballast for bad weather. They make a big show and have great pretensions but they have no reserve. They are not reliable in an emergency. They lack stability.

The great problem of the racing yacht builder is to secure the greatest possible speed consistent with safety. The lines of the boat must not only be constructed to provide the least possible resistance to the water but also to provide against the possibility of capsizing in sudden squalls or a heavy sea.

Every person ought to be able to rely upon good sense and good judgment to keep them steady in any emergency. If you wish to keep your head and not crumble in stress situations you must cultivate a practical frame of mind. Only then can you hope to keep cool no matter what happens. The compass of one's judgment must point as true in a storm as in the sunshine. It can do so only if one is consistent in one's thinking.

There are certain plants and trees which kill every other growing thing in their neighborhood. They poison the soil surface and plants around them which stunts the growth of those species of vegetation sensitive to their sap, leaves or bark. Some employers so poison their environment that even the most capable employees cannot prosper under them. They seem to have a perfect genius for dampening the enthusiasm and spontaneity of their employees who shrivel and shrink every time they come near them. They make it very difficult for their employees to take an interest in their welfare because the employer belittles them, scolds them, and takes the heart out of the employee all the time.

They do not praise the principle. Their atmosphere is so suffocating, so depressing, that those about them feel unable to act naturally in their presence or do themselves justice. They feel nervous and ill at ease. I have known of employees who worked years in such an atmosphere without getting ahead. They thought it was lack of ability that kept them down but when they changed their employers and got into a congenial environment they advanced rapidly. They expanded like tropical plants which had been stunted for a time in a cold climate but which flourished when taken back to their native soil. Some people are so constituted that they live for praise and appreciation. They cannot do good work without it. There is nothing that will stimulate the average employee to work harder than commendation or an expression of appreciation. The fact is nothing else will so bind employees to their employer as the feeling that they are appreciated. Nothing will so encourage them as a word of praise when they try to do their best.

Do not be afraid to praise heartily. Do not give pinched, stinted appreciation, as though you were afraid to spoil your employees. Be whole-hearted and generous in your praise. You will be surprised to see how they will respond. Many a successful man and woman have found the turning-points of their careers in a little praise a little hopeful encouragement. They date their first step upward from an encouraging letter expressing appreciation of something they did or a simple word of praise which kindled hope or aroused the ambition and determination to be somebody effective in the world.

No one can be original, creative, and prolific in their work when they are afraid or feel suppressed. Spontaneity and flexibility are absolutely necessary for the best results. If your employees are hemmed in, watched, suspected or criticized their work will be an inferior quality. Optimism and hope are powerful agents of excellence and industry.

Fault-finding is, after penny-pinching, the most shortsighted policy in the world. It is energy wasted. When a person makes a mistake, speak to them kindly and not in front of others. It will work magic. Never lose an opportunity for showing your appreciation of a good piece of work.

It pays to keep employees contented and happy. It increases their productivity and the quality of their service as well as improving the general work situation.

If your employees feel that you care only for what you can get out of them they will feel the same way about you and care only for their salaries and for an easy time.

Their respect and admiration are worth everything to you. They hold your success or failure largely in their hands. They can often turn the tide and make all the difference between good fortune and bad.

In short, the test of a well-balanced person is that they do not change with changed conditions. Financial losses, failure, sorrow, do not throw them off-balance. Nor are they puffed up by a little prosperity.

Chapter 12

The Power of Positive Thinking and Tenacity

There is nothing less useful or more depressing than dwelling upon lost opportunities or a misspent life.

Whatever your past has been, forget it.

If it throws a shadow on the present, if you can find nothing in it which helps you, there is not a single reason why you should retain it in your memory once you have thoroughly assessed the effects of misfortune upon your character and personality. Was some defect of yours responsible for your bad times? If not, let bygones be bygones.

Nothing is more destructive than dragging memories of foolish deeds and unfortunate experiences of the past into today's work to mar and spoil it. There are plenty of people who have been failures up to the present moment who could do wonders in the future if only they could forget the past, close the door on it forever and start anew.

I know a number of people who complain of their wretched fate and hard luck who are, themselves, their own worst enemies. Unconsciously, they poison and devitalize the atmosphere of their surroundings by the image or failure which they are constantly envisioning in their minds. Their pessimism, exhaling from every pore, envelops them in a dense but invisible atmosphere through which no ray of light or hope can penetrate—and yet they wonder why they do not succeed. They expect brightness to arise from darkness, hope from despair and cheer from gloom.

These same people would think a farmer ridiculous who would sow nettle seeds and expect them to produce wheat or corn or one who should plant deadly weeds in his garden and expect to see roses or lilies flourishing on the spot. They do not seem to appreciate the fact that everywhere in the universe like produces like. Whatever thought we sow, we must reap in kind. The sour, gloomy, pessimistic seed sown in the garden of the mind must produce its own peculiar fruit. Grapes will not grow on thorns or figs on thistles.

The man or woman who exhausts himself in complaining, who is always protesting that there is no justice in the world, that merit is not rewarded, that the times are out of joint and that everything is wrong, is usually put down as a weak person or a small petty complainer. Large-minded men and women do not spend their energies whining and complaining. If they meet an obstacle they go around it and get on about their business. They know that all their time and strength must be concentrated on the work of making a life. The whiner not only wastes their time and strength but they prejudice people against them. No one feels inclined to help a person who is always complaining of conditions and blaming their "hard luck." Somehow, we have a feeling that they deserve what they got.

Practical business people often have no sympathy with the person who claims that he cannot get a job. Prospective employers object to having people around who complain that "luck has always been against them." The employee is usually no more extraordinary than other people but the employer fears, perhaps not without reason, that they will bring their bad luck with them.

For example, I once heard of an English businessman politician who advertised for a butler. He wanted a combination of valet and companion. He had reduced the number of applicants for the position to a single person, and was about to complete his arrangements when the man began to tell of his career, his thwarted ambitions and his misfortunes. It was a genuine "hard-luck" story. The politician listened for a while and then astonished his would-be employee by saying, "I find I do not want you". When urged to give his reasons for the sudden change in his decision, he replied, "I never hire 'hard-luck' people, especially the kind who talk about it." His decision may seem shallow and even brutal. The prospective valet may not have even been responsible for his bad luck and he might have made a valuable servant. But, putting aside the question of the justice or astuteness of the particular decision, we can see that the story points up the fact that in a job interview the complainer puts themself at a fearful disadvantage by their own conduct.

People are so constituted that they do their best work when they are not preoccupied with their troubles and when they are basically contented and at ease. Remember that discord is always an enemy to achievement as well as to one's comfort and happiness. It whittles away at whatever store of vitality and energy we have.

When the mind is full of discord, worry and anxiety and when brain and body are out of tune, it is impossible even for a genius at living to show the potential of a full free life. People do not realize the degree to which their energy is wasted in friction worry and anxiety. How many people completely exhaust themselves in needless worrying and bickering over things which are not worthwhile! How many burn up their energy and waste their time in useless activities from temper tantrums to systemless work in a hundred different moments each day. Think how much they could accomplish with a little thought and attention to the delicate human instrument on which we are playing!

If a young person should begin to draw out of the bank the money which they had been saving for years for the purpose of going into business for themself and if they should begin to fritter it away on useless expenditures we would regard them as very foolish and predict their failure. But many of us throw away our own success and happiness just as foolishly in friction. We cannot do two things at once with our energy. If we use it up in friction we cannot expend it in effective work.

Many people whose lives have been failures could have accomplished great things if they could only have kept themselves detached from the friction, worry and anxiety of their daily routine. A fundamental cheerfulness enables one to do this. Every muscle and every nerve must be tuned to express it. If the idea of "working at" cheerfulness does not appeal to you consider how essential to music the preliminary tuning of the instruments is. As the piano tuner eliminates the least discord in sound so the successful person tunes out the discordant notes of passion, hatred, jealousy and worry in their personality. The mature person would no more think of starting their day cross and fractious than a great master musician would think of playing in public on an instrument that was out of tune.

Gloom, despondency, worry about the future and all discordant passion can be tuned out of your life by planning and constructing the future rather than brooding about the past.

This does not mean that you must carefully anticipate each day's activities, rehearse them, and finally accomplish them after having wasted three times as much effort on them as is necessary. Rather, strategic planning is what is called for each day. You must develop a sense of the pressure of each day's events and respond to that pressure with flexibility. "Efficiency experts" have been made figures of fun by comedians when they appear to waste more time devising the proper way of doing things than in actually doing them. They know that this is sometimes necessary but true efficiency resides in elasticity, as opposed to automatism. Elasticity, in turn, is the product of mental health, environmental challenge, and a problem-solving mentality.

Many people start out in life with great enthusiasm which generally oozes away before they reach their goal. All along life's course we see people who have dropped out of the running at different stages. They may be industrious, honest, enthusiastic, well-educated and have had good opportunities but they lack persistence and courage and withdraw from the race when the unseen goal is not far off.

An army which no human being might care to number lies encamped around the great city of Success, close to its walls, near to its very gates, but they have never entered the city and they never will enter it. Thousands of people in this great army of the defeated would tell you, if questioned, that they never had a fair chance. Usually because their education was neglected or because they never had anyone to favor them or they lacked the tenacity and persistence necessary for success. Yet many of them could have taken advantage of night schools and great public libraries in their evenings and other free time. Abe Lincoln and others who rose from humble origins to success marched past such people with triumphant steps on their way to victory because they persisted in adversity.

Nearly every successful person has felt, during years of struggle and endeavour, that they were accomplishing very little and that they might fail in life. But those who have succeeded kept on trying no matter how great the obstacles in their path to achievement. There is no genius like that of holding on and of striving in difficult circumstances.

There are thousands of people who have talent of one sort or another but few who have "True grit." Brilliance and talent alone cannot achieve success. In public life, there are some brilliant people who fall short of doing great things. People who raise great expectations in some particular line, but who never fulfill these expectations. They remain perpetually "untapped potential."

More people fail from the lack of staying power than from almost anything else.

There is another aspect to persistence. Many people are willing to pay any price to attain their ambitions except that of plain hard work. They are willing to expend any amount of energy in scheming, in devising short-cuts and abridged methods and in constructing cunning devices but the thought of many years of tedious labor or of sacrificing a thousand and one little comforts and pleasures seem to be too much for them.

It seems that lots of people spend many precious years trying to find "bargains" in success, "marked down" achievements and quicker methods than hard work.

Some people have the peculiar faculty of pushing things through and getting things done. This is always a sign of strength and of creative ability and an indication of leadership.

Almost anybody can start something but it is a rare person who can carry everything they undertake to a finish.

Chapter 13

Authority

A stranger going into a big business establishment might get the impression that the hundreds of employees hurrying and scurrying about and doing a great deal of talking and bustling were responsible for the enormous volume of business being done. But if they could go into certain private offices in the establishment they would probably find sitting there a few quiet, serene, level-headed people who with relatively few words dominate and control all the activities of the hundreds and thousands of employees. They are the moving force behind all the hurry, bustle and show.

The person who aspires to leadership must be an organizer. They must be able not only to assess people but to judge accurately what to do with them and how to place and measure them. It has to be easy for them to dominate without antagonizing, to handle the responsibility of their position without timidity.

It seems natural and easy for some people to lead with

confidence and respect. Employees must see that the leader is businesslike and has executive ability. Then they will follow The Leader with zeal and loyalty. Creating a great enterprise requires the ability to handle people, an ability which arises from a certain capacity for the sympathetic intuition of human needs.

The greatest leaders are those who combine executive ability with kindness and consideration. Employees will follow such a leader enthusiastically and work for them nights and holidays. They will do anything to help The Leader along. If they see nothing in the leader to admire, they may follow and if they see nothing to respect they may take orders but they will do so in the lifeless manner of mere wage slaves.

It is unreasonable for an employer to expect to arouse in his or her employees qualities which are vastly superior to the qualities the employer them self possesses. The essential qualities which characterize a person of authority and which qualify one for any position of responsibility are superiority in one's field and the force of character with the ability to delegate and the ability to plan and push through any undertaking to the finish.

If you are afraid of making enemies do not try to lead. For the moment you step out of the crowd and show originality or individuality you will be criticized, condemned and caricatured. Some people find it irresistible to throw stones at the head lifted above the crowd. No great leader has yet escaped the jealousy and envy of those who did not keep up with them or do what they did. A leader must be positive and aggressive. They must be as inflexible in their purpose as they are elastic in discovering the means to accomplish it. They must at times exhibit boldness bordering on audacity. They must be able to withstand criticism without being insensible or indifferent to it. A certain toughness, which is not contradictory to an awareness of the feelings of others, characterizes the person who is potentially a leader.

Some of our greatest leaders have been extremely sensitive to criticism. Censure was very painful to them yet they were able to carry on in spite of the pain caused by harsh judgment and unjust condemnation. Many worthy young people have retired from the race for leadership because of the sting inflicted by the malicious and envious comments of their fellows. They did not think the honey worth the sting.

Bureaucratic leadership today calls for great breadth of vision in addition to the same general qualities which made the leader of the past. The vast corporations and the enormous interests involved in our large businesses today require a knowledge of corporate economy, law, hiring practices, etc. It is a host of specialized and interrelated disciplines. Expertise in organization tactics is essential for the executive who aspires to go to the top of corporate management. There never was such a need as there is today for persons who can perceive the effects of business on people, both employees and the public at large.

The collective method of education destroys individuality except in cases where special talents and characteristics are so marked that they cannot be dulled or blunted by any amount of conventional training. It nips originality in the bud and tends to make the child an imitator or timid observer of life instead of an original, forceful and distinct participant. The dreamy bookworm, the matter-of-fact realist, the inventive spirit, the introspective contemplative, those with the brain of a financier, and those who delight in mimic warfare and strategic games are all are put into the same mold and subjected to the same processes. The result is, inevitably, that nine-tenths of the children educated in this mechanistic fashion arc carbon copies of the same pattern. A great many people of executive potential become followers of others and echoes instead of inventors of discourse because their distinctive qualities were not developed or encouraged in youth.

It is sad to see people seeking the advice of others when they are amply able to give advice. They are never daring to venture on their own or rely on their own judgment because they have always leaned upon others or depended upon someone else to lead the way! Their strongest inherent qualities, their common sense and independence of mind, lie dormant within them. They are operating at half their efficiency solely because of a lack of training for their particular role.

True education promotes the flowering of possibilities, fosters self-reliance, encourages and stimulates initiative and executive ability. Education is as much process as it is input. It should provide for the cultivation of all the faculties, exercising, strengthening and buttressing them.

We want our young people to be so educated that their qualities of leadership, their originality, and their individuality will be emphasized and strengthened instead of obliterated.

The qualities which make a great leader are necessary for every achiever to acquire. Self-assurance, a spirit of independence, courage, and maturity are developed by the demands of life and work from youth onwards. Scores of college graduates who have won their diplomas legitimately and honorably fail hopelessly when they attempt to grapple with the practical side of life. They have no qualities of leadership, no independence of thought, and no self-reliance. They are filled with facts and figures, theories and plans but they are unable to put their theoretical knowledge to practical use. When required to carry on the business of their profession they fall into the patterns established by their predecessors. They have not been trained to cut through the bureaucratic red tape which hampers executive decision-making or to exercise their ingenuity in manipulating conventional situations with more than ordinary flair and dexterity.

It is the ability to get things done, to achieve, that is necessary in the executive position. You can always count on advisors and information experts and specialists to help you make informed decisions. Remember that your chief asset as an executive is your ability to orchestrate the entire event or production that is at hand. Have confidence in your practical ability to deal with conditions rather than theories. If you are known as a person who "gets results," you will be in demand everywhere.

Education is not stuffing the mind with facts and theories until it becomes an unwieldy lexicon of possibilities. Truly well educated persons are not loaded down with text-book information that they cannot put to use. The truly well-educated person has developed their faculties of inquiry and judgment to such an extent that they will never be a, imitator, or follower. They may not necessarily be a great leader but they will not derive their opinions solely from others. They will trust their own judgment, "be themselves," and live their own life wherever they find themselves.

The essential quality of the mind of most leaders is a pragmatic ingenuity and a certain directness which enables them to put their knowledge to use. This quality is not brought out or developed by schooling but by experience and responsibility.

Chapter 14

The Importance of Education

Although several negative things have been said so far about contemporary education it should be clear that nothing is more important than attaining both adequate training in one's field and a broad educational background. The habit of acquiring information and practical wisdom is developed at school and early in life. It is not by leaps and bounds but by steady persistent growth that strong characters are shaped. They mature with training and discipline.

Great ends cannot be achieved all at once. It is the persistent attempt to enlarge and broaden the horizon of our knowledge by good reading, by constant study, and by perpetual inquiry that enables us to excel.

We cannot help believing in the child who is always trying to improve them self who takes advantage of every opportunity to make them self a little better informed. They are attracted to good reading and are always asking questions, observing, and trying to get an education. Such eagerness to improve them self indicates their superiority and their staying power. Ambivalent, lazy and indifferent children prefer "a good time" to acquiring knowledge. They are not willing to give up their play for the sake of acquiring skills or increasing knowledge.

We all miss opportunities for self-improvement and for training our mind and heart in every day life. There is a kind of art to being able to perceive such opportunities no matter what your occupation may be. If we form the habit of good critical reading and intelligent conversation and entertainment that stimulates the mind we will have the secret of perpetual growth.

Nothing else will give you greater satisfaction later in life than the forming of systematic habits of self-culture early in life. Your self improvement processes will become automatic. If you do that it becomes just as natural for you to use every bit of leisure time for reading something helpful or useful as it is for you to breathe.

I know a young man who travels a great deal. He always carries with him a bit of good reading. Wherever he goes he has something with him whether miniature classics or correspondence school lessons. This fellow is always doing something to improve himself in the odds and ends of time which most people throw away. The result is that he is well informed upon a great variety of subjects. He is widely read in history in English literature and in popular science.

Modern electronic devices now make it so you can carry hundreds of books with you and the devices are lightweight and easy to read. You can also download books to these readers while standing on the street. So there is no excuse for not having good reading material anywhere and at any time.

What this man has accomplished in his leisure is a rebuke to those who waste all their time in doing nothing or in doing that which is worse than nothing. You cannot realize the inestimable value of time spent in good reading or some other form of self-improvement. Did you ever realize that scores of people have given themselves the equivalent of a college education in their spare moments and long evenings? You might as well say that there is no use in trying to save anything from your small salary or income as it is to say that you can never get a liberal education by studying during your spare time. Every bit of knowledge you store up enriches your life, increases your expertise and makes you better able to cope with life. You can never make a better investment than by forming the habit of good reading. It will multiply your efficiency, give you the power to break away from your environment and throw off the yoke of dependence which galls you. It will make you more independent and self-reliant. Higher education will also bolster your confidence in yourself. In addition to all this if your knowledge is practical and you use it wisely it will enable you to have a better opinion of yourself as a man or woman.

There never was a time in known history when education was worth so much as it is today both with respect to technical expertise and humanistic understanding. Competition has become so terrific and life so complex that one needs to be armed with every variety of expertise possible. The greatest favor you can do yourself in the world is to broaden your field of practical knowledge. There is no gift which you can give to the world like that of a productive manhood or womanhood. You can do nothing better than this.

What a golden opportunity confronts you for turning your leisure into knowledge. It will mean growth of character as well as promotion, advancement and security that no accident can take from you and no disaster annihilate.

No matter how small your salary may be, never underestimate the value of every bit of valuable information you pick up and every bit of genuine reading you do or reflective thinking you engage yourself in. I have known youths working very hard for very little money to do more for their advancement by improving their minds in their spare time and days off from work than by the actual work they did. Their salaries were in-

significant in comparison with the self education they managed
to acquire.

I know a man who doubled his salary in one bound largely
because of his insatiable efforts at self-improvement. His great
passion seemed to be to become as well-rounded a man as possible. This young man is a good example of the importance of
establishing your reputation in the world. Everybody who knew
him knew that he was determined to make something of himself. His fellow employees soon found that it was impossible to
tease him away from his reading or studying because he had his
eyes on the future. He had rejected a modest future of limited
prospects and was not content with a barren self-image. He
had a passion for new knowledge. Those who worked with him
were surprised at his rapid advancement but there was a good
reason for it. While they were spending their evenings and
money having a good time he was educating himself in a rigid
course of self-improvement.

Everywhere we see young men and women of executive
potential continue in very ordinary jobs without advancement
simply because, though they are intelligent, they were never
properly trained. They have never tried to improve their general knowledge or literacy by good reading or by extending
their interests. Their salaries when they were paid and a good
time after work are about all they looked forward to during the
week. This low level of anticipation in life takes its toll in dull
careers. Men and women who have utilized only a very small
percentage of their ability, who have not been disciplined by
responsibility and educated by experience, always work at a
disadvantage. A person capable of being an employer is often
compelled by circumstances to be a very ordinary employee.
This has effects on his or her personality as well as productivity.

One of the greatest questions that faces you when you are
dissatisfied with your job is will you take advantage of alter-
native or so-called adult education. Because the commercial

opportunities and prizes are so great in this country young people catch the money-making disease early and are impatient to get an early start in the job-market. Many of them cannot see the use of years of drudgery in school and college. They have neither the experience nor the judgment to realize the infinite value of a well-stored mind. Because of their inexperience they do not realize the tremendous handicap ignorance will prove to be in their later careers when they come to compete with people of superior education and training.

Unless youths are fortunate enough to have parents or advisors who have fitted them to enter the battle of the strong they quit college before getting their degree or even leave school before obtaining their high-school diploma and start out in life half-prepared. Only later do they see their terrible mistake and usually without making any special effort to compensate for their loss. Unfortunately most adults have the impression that once they have passed the easily educable period of their youth they can never acquire the necessity of a broader education. Yet, there is a way.

The adult education system provides a perfectly practical means by which adults can, even while continuing in business, get a good education. Misconceptions about the possible value of adult education programs are due to a variety of factors. It is not as easy later in life as it is in childhood to commit new information to memory. Hence languages, mathematics, and other elementary disciplines are learned more slowly by adults than by children. On the other hand, the analytic faculties of adults are more fully developed because they have already been sharpened by experience and the exercise of practical judgement.

Once adults have decided that they want further education they can work harder and are generally willing to make greater sacrifices in order to compensate for their lacks. They know the relative value for them of their new education and they are much more practical in gaining their training. They are more eager to learn especially after they have advanced enough to see the benefits of their newly acquired knowledge. There are many people eager for new proficiency who do not know how to begin to acquire an education that will be practical and comparatively easy to obtain in their spare time or during their evenings.

Most people are incapable of self-direction or systematic study. They need instructors who will direct them and encourage them and keep them at work until they have acquired the habits of concentration and attentive study. On the other hand some very able men and women have obtained most of their education by reading alone. Although they have attended very little school, by persistent reading they have become well-educated in history, politics, literature and philosophy and acquired all sorts of needed training. They have achieved all of this during their evenings and odd moments which most people either throw away or spend in pursuing pleasure.

The pursuit of learning by one who is hungry for knowledge provides the highest kind of pleasure in addition to bestowing discipline and expertise upon them. Thus it is inspiring to see an adult seizing every opportunity to make up for the loss of early educational advantages and pouring their soul into their spare moments and evenings, trying to make them self a more fully educated person.

Getting an education is like acquiring a fortune. In itself, a little savings does not amount to much. It must be invested in order to increase. People tend to spend a small savings because it does not appear to be the foundation of a fortune and so they keep spending and do not acquire a fortune. Many adults who feel the need to make up for their early educational losses do not think that a few minutes of reading during their spare time will accomplish much. Yet this is precisely the way to acquire an extremely serviceable substitute for college courses especially if one has the direction of a licensed school.

Do not throw away the opportunity for learning as so many others have thoughtlessly done. Education is power.

Chapter 15

The Habit of Ambition

"What are the motives which impel a person to keep slaving after they have acquired a livelihood? Is all ambition selfish?" These and similar questions are frequently asked.

The passion for power and the love of achievement are among the most important characteristics of human nature. With most people food, shelter and a steady job are not the motives for an active career. Career orientation comes from different sources.

Even if we are only dimly conscious that we owe something to the world, within each of us there is something which protests against our living idle purposeless lives. There is something which tells us that our debt to the human race is a personal one. A sufficiently strong ego tells us that our individual duty as a social creature is not transferable and any message we may have for humanity we must deliver ourselves. We should never feel right unless in some fashion we are doing our part of the world's work. We should never wish to be drones in the great human experience or to eat, drink, wear and use what others have produced without contributing to the general well-being of our society.

It is difficult for many people at this time to have a sense of the importance of their role in life. Yet we should feel that it is unworthy of us not to seek a mature role in life; the prospect of sitting around should violate our sense of justice and fairness. Despite the seemingly set pattern of their lives, all normal men and women occasionally feel the yearning for a fuller, more complete life. The craving for expansion, for growth and the desire to actualize our dreams and give birth to our ideas and the aspiration to exercise our inventiveness and ingenuity—these are the compelling motives for a creative career.

A person fulfills their social role through their inventive ability and their ability to provide their fellows with that which will emancipate them from drudgery. Another person delivers their message through their art or handiwork and another through science and another through their gift with words. All the modes of human expression are opportunities for benefitting our society and our world. In every ambitious career, the motivating force goes beyond the mere need to earn a living.

The great artists do not paint simply for a living, but because they must express something that is struggling for expression. They have an irresistible desire to express visibly a felt relation. We all long to bring out the ideal, whatever it may be, that lives within us. We ourselves often do not know what it is until we attempt to express it and we want the world to see it.

It is not always goal-orientation so much as the inherent passion in most people for achievement and self-assertion that urges us on. This is what keeps us struggling to achieve even when we have accomplished a specific goal.

Some primitive tribes believe that the spirit of their conquered enemies enters into the members of their own community and strengthens them. In our view of the psychological battles of contemporary living we perceive every business or professional conquest and every financial victory and every triumph over obstacles in our daily routine as producing a measurably larger and more confident person.

The exercise of the creative faculties to meet the challenge of problem-solving constitutes a powerful mental tonic and gives immense satisfaction. Think of the tameness, the mental flabbiness of the lives of inactive and purposeless persons who have neither something special to do nor a vision of the importance of the sort of work they in fact do! Compare their lives with that of a person who feels all the forces within them heaving and tugging away to accomplish a mighty purpose!

The idle aimless person does not know the meaning of personal power or the satisfaction which comes to the doer, the achiever. If you wonder why people who have already made a living continue to struggle or to engage in strenuous competition with as much zeal and ardor as ever when they might retire from the field then you do not realize the tremendous fascination of the game itself especially for those with inventiveness and authority.

We might just as well wonder why great artists and authors, singers, actors and other performers do not retire from activity and give up their work when they are at the zenith of their power. They have just arrived at the position in which they can give their greatest performances. Do you wonder why great business men and women or professionals do not retire in the most fruitful period of their lives merely because they have made their living?

The unborn creatures of the artist's imagination struggle for expression and haunt them until they are made real. So, too, the ambitions and ideals of the business person or professional clamor for expression during their entire career. Those who have never won major battles in business do not realize what a deep hold this passion for winning has for the achiever or how it grips them and encourages them and nerves them for greater triumphs.

A great business person develops the same lust for power that possessed Napoleon or other military figures. For some persons the desire to achieve and to dominate grows stronger and more vigorous with every new victory. The ambition for greater achievement which years of winning have strengthened often becomes abnormal so that people who have grown accustomed to wielding enormous power shudder at the very thought of laying down the scepter. Think of the business potentates of the world whose power governs vast fields of activity—think of these people retiring merely because they have acquired sufficient gains to make them comfortable for the rest of their lives.

Frequently people change career in middle life after they have been in a certain line of business or profession for many years. Their new occupation has greater intrinsic appeal than the job in which they found themselves for numbers of years. Seldom is the change made for financial reasons alone. Greater challenges, closer ties to their personal interests, greater possibilities for improving the quality of their work-life—all these are reasons which compel people to change their profession.

We hear a great deal of criticism of the greed and insensitivity of the rich which keeps them pushing ahead after they have acquired more money than they can ever use. A distinction must be made between greed and the spirit of enterprise. Many of these people find their reward in the exercise of their powers and not in amassing money. Greed plays a comparatively small part in their struggle for conquest. This is not true of all rich people, of course. Many of them are in business solely for the love of accumulating. Their selfishness and greed have been indulged for so long that it amounts to a passion. But the fully developed person who has chosen the world of business as their arena for the love of achievement satisfies their sense of duty and justice within that world and becomes a larger more complete person. They "plays the game" for the training it gives and for the opportunity of self-expression that it provides. They seize all opportunities for improving the world in which they find themself using the power of their position to overcome rather than perpetuate the evils of "the system".

The tyranny of habit, while not a motive force, is also a powerful factor in keeping people going. The daily routine of our business or professional world becomes a part of the rhythm of our very lives. When we have become accustomed to doing the same things every day for a quarter or half a century, then radical change is neither a pleasant thing to contemplate or an easy thing to endure. Every normal person dreads retirement and fears the shrinking and shriveling which inevitably follow the change from an active to an inactive life. To many, retirement appears a sort of slow suicide during which a gradual atrophy of their talents and powers takes place. Retirement need not be inactive, of course, and should not be feared as an empty time in which one prepares to die. New interests and the resurrection of old undeveloped faculties can enliven retirement years and reveal a more complete personality.

There are many reasons why people do not retire entirely from the active world as soon as he or she can. A whole life's momentum and the grip of habit, which increases facility and desire at every repetition tend to keep people in business in their chosen occupations or in new lines of endeavour. It is the love of forging ahead, of advancing into new fields, and of meeting the challenges we perceive in our chosen fields, not greed or selfishness, that keeps most of us working.

Many people in business or the professions and some artists as well are like the mountain climbers who will endure all sorts of hardships in the pursuit of the conquest but who loses interest shortly after they reach the summit. The love of achievement is satisfied in the very act of creation, in the realization of the ideal which had haunted the brain. Ease, leisure, and comfort are nothing compared with the exhilaration which comes from achievement. Who can describe the sense of triumph that fills the inventor, the joy that thrills them when they first see produced a mechanism or device—their own handiwork— which will free people from labor?

Imagine the satisfaction of the scientist who after years of battling with poverty, criticism, and denunciation and per- haps the tortures of being misunderstood by those dearest to them finally succeeds at last in their research. The struggle for achievement, the mastery of nature's secrets, the conquest of obstacles, the triumph of ideals has created what we call prog- ress. It has at times brought out the finest and noblest traits in human nature and broadened and strengthened the vision of excellence by which people build their culture.

Every normal human being is born with a sacred obliga- tion resting on them: that of using their faculties for the highest purposes possible and of giving their best to the world.

The laws of human nature and of the universe are such that the more one gives to the world, the more one gets back and the more complete a person becomes.

But the moment people become victims of selfishness, greed and self-indulgence they become smaller and they de- mean themselves. It is no wonder that the person who retires merely for selfish reasons is uneasy, unhappy and sometimes suicidal. They know in their heart that it is wrong to withdraw their productive and creative ability from a world that needs it so much. They feel that it is a sin against their own develop- ment and their still future possibilities to cease from activity in a world they have helped construct.

If we could analyze a strong vigorous character we would find it is typified by the habit of overcoming obstacles. By the same token if we should analyze its antithesis, the weak charac- ter, we should find the habit of letting things slide and of yield- ing instead of conquering and the lack of courage, persistence, and grit.

There is a great difference between the self-made person and a pampered youth who has never been confronted by situations that might exercise their powers of ingenuity, daring, and persistence. It is the difference between the stalwart oak which has been battered by the storm and the hothouse plant which has never been allowed to feel a breath of frost or a rough wind.

Every bit of the oak's fibre has registered a victory and therefore we seek its timber to endure exposure to the elements and the predations of time. Unlike the hothouse plant the wild oak's trunk and its branches will not succumb to the first adverse wind. Responsible people are like that too. They do not crumble before adversity because their inner fibre has been developed and strengthened. Responsibility itself is a powerful developing factor which the idle aimless person never gets the advantage to experience. Great responsibilities bring out great reserves to match them.

The thought of being able to benefit mankind has held many people to idealistic pursuits amid suffering, hardship, and overwhelming difficulties. Normal human beings are happiest when doing that which best suits them, that which they are best fitted to do and when they are trying to actualize their own vision of excellence. They are weakest and most miserable when idle or doing that for which they are least fitted by nature.

The divine discontent which all aspiring souls feel at times is a longing for growth and for a realization of their possibilities.

It is the longing from within for that expansion and power which can only come from the vigorous pursuit of worthy aims. There is no mental tonic and no physical stimulus like that which comes from the consciousness of growing fuller and more complete each day in the pursuit of honorable goals.

The passion for achievement becomes strong and powerful when it has legitimate exercise and encouragement.

Every exercise of one's faculties today enlarges the possibilities of tomorrow.

Chapter 16

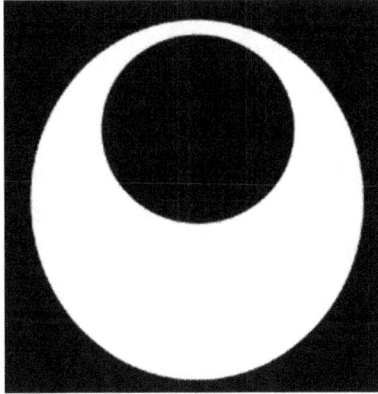

Mother

At the risk of over-generalizing, one may say that what has been true in centuries past is not necessarily the case today. Very few people can say, with Abe Lincoln, "I owe it all to my angel mother."

Yet the testimony of great people in acknowledgment of their mothers' boundless aid and affection would make a record stretching from the dawn of history up to the present. It has been said that few people become great who do not owe their stature at least in part to a mother's love and inspiration. The problem in this age is that mothers have been taught to advance their children's careers or prospects at the expense of their own character. The influence of Mother is still great and still accomplishes good: "I never could have reached my present position had I not known that my mother expected me to do so," says one successful politician. "From my earliest child-hood, my mother made me feel that I was born for this occupa-

tion and that it was my vocation in life. Her life faith spurred
me on and gave me the power to create", says a distinguished
professional. Yet the ties between success and motherhood are
often hidden and ineffectual in this age. The common celebration of motherhood on Mother's Day is the only way we have
of expressing some gratitude for the relation that is the source
of our culture's stability. Family sentiment, like religious feeling, is too unsophisticated for us. Perhaps those who object
to sentimentalizing the relation of mother and child are right.
How many people can say "In my mother's presence I become
for the time transformed into another being." Those who have
felt a truly maternal love know the truth of this statement. Yet
maternal tenderness and strength are not fostered in our culture.

It is not that women are unappreciated, exactly. The hostil-
ity against her in the job market is being mitigated by legisla-
tion and open hiring practices, etc. Yet the duplicity of poor
Mother's role as siren, wonder woman, and breadwinner has
taken its toll on her essential, if not universal, identity. She is
no longer appreciated as mother. She no longer appreciates
herself in this profoundly archetypal and pure role.

Our mothers are the molders of the world today though they
get little credit for their work and little praise and little blame.
The world sees only the successful child and the mother is but
a rung in the ladder upon which they have climbed. Her name
is seldom reported in the newspapers although we do our best
to praise women who have achieved some mark of distinction
while keeping their familial roles intact. We have even set aside
one day a year in which to honor our mothers. We are fond of
stories of success in which Mother is praised and we feel that
it is right that the material success of an individual had psychological sources rooted in familial love. "My mother was the
making of me", said Thomas Edison once. "She was so true, so
sure of me; and I felt that I had someone to live for; someone I
must not disappoint." We are all aware of the power of encour-

agement from our elders. "A kiss from my mother made me a painter", said Benjamin West.

Yet few people understand how difficult it is for mothers today to perform their ministries as living example, heroine, disciplinarian and advisor. Their mothers had difficulties also. The effects of two world wars and many other destroyers of family ties may seem insignificant yet they are not because the seeds of disorientation sown then have been reseeding themselves under new pressures of the modern era. The deterioration of the home, of maternity and paternity, have promoted a loss of old standards.

Heroism still abounds. I know a mother who has brought up a large family of children under conditions which, I believe, no man living could have possibly survived. She had a lazy worthless husband with no ambition or force of character. He was a man who was extremely selfish and exacting and who not only did practically nothing to help his wife carry her terrible burdens but also insisted upon her catering to his whims. He would not lift a finger to help her, if he could avoid it, and would leave her in the lurch at the moments when she most needed the presence of a supportive adult. When the children were sick and when she was behind in her work. He was a good dresser and she had no time or money for clothes. How complex a situation for children when Mother does not know how to demand what is her due!

Some feminine heroism is more happily rewarded. I once saw a splendid young college graduate introduce his poor plainly dressed old mother to his classmates with as much pride and dignity as though she were a queen. Her form was bent and she appeared prematurely aged by her cares. Yet her face glowed with the mutual love and pride which she and her son shared. Who but a mother would make such sacrifices as she clearly had, draining all her energy for her children and yet never asking for or expecting compensation?

There is no one in the average family whose services begin to compare with those of the mother and yet no one is more generally neglected or exploited. A certain innocence characterizes the maternal role. It is free of shrewdness and therefore open to attack. This does not mean that the maternal personality lacks shrewdness in every respect. Homemakers are required to conduct economic practices that would tax the ingenuity of a degreed expert. Today, besides the responsibility of house and home, the mother has the added duty of self-education. Without training she feels she cannot cope with the problems facing her and her child today.

No matter how loving or thoughtful the working parent may be, the heavier burdens and the weightier responsibilities of child-rearing always fall on the parent who remains in the home which is usually the mother. The virtues of a good mother are a constant temptation to the other members of the family, especially the selfish ones, to take advantage. If she were not so kind, so affectionate and tender, so generous and ever ready to make all sorts of sacrifices for others; if she were not so willing to efface herself; if she were more self-assertive; if, in short, she demanded her rights as a person, she would have a much easier time.

These days many women do demand of their families that they be regarded as full persons with needs of their own and tastes of their own with skills outside those required to care for the home and family. Surely this is a step in the right direction. But wouldn't it be wonderful if greater appreciation could be extended towards mothers?

In the age when television brings a variety of social viewpoints into the home for hours each day you would think children could be given a feeling of respect for the honest hardworking tasks of homemaking. Mother, in turn, should be able to feel her position of authority reinforced by society but this is not so. The break-down of the family, if it is accomplished, will be from within and it will be due to misguided motherhood more than outside pressures.

Not long ago a mother, one whose sufferings and sacrifices for her children during a long and terrible struggle with poverty should have been acknowledged with a monument, told me that "she guessed she'd better go to the old folks' home and end her days there." What a picture that was! An old lady with white hair and a sweet beautiful face, with a wonderful light in her eye who was calm, serene, patient and dignified has her children, all of whom are married and successful, make her feel as if she were a burden. She had no home other own, not a single stick of furniture, none of the things that are so dear to everyone. This old woman, who, in order to bring up half a dozen children, had made sacrifices that were simply heart-rending, received in her old age only a small monthly allowance from her prosperous sons. They apparently never thought about the joy it might give her to own her own home and to possess some pretty furnishings and a few pictures.

I am acquainted with another mother who is obliged to ask her well-to-do children for everything she has in the way of clothing. She is so sensitive and feels so humiliated because of her dependence that she waits until her own sense of decency and self-respect forces her practically to beg from her children.

Although the social security benefits for the elderly today are supposed, in some fashion, to compensate for the breakdown of strong family ties as well as the reduction of income through retirement, they seldom provide the elderly with a livelihood. Maudlin as the above stories may sound to some ears, there are greater outrages enacted today against the elderly. The core problem is a lack of family commitment. Because of the change, often quite radical, in loyalties and orientation many children when grown forget their early ties and feel that they have left their commitment to family.

Because of the dissolution of early ties and because sometimes such ties were never felt in the first place and because in many cases people are the victims of simple thoughtlessness and a lack of imagination, children do not as a rule provide generously for their elderly relations. Yet by denying their parents the complement of their own youth and vitality, they deprive themselves of a whole dimension of human life.

A president of France, even after his elevation to the highest executive position, took great pride in visiting his mother who was a humble market gardener in a little French village. A writer on one occasion described a meeting between this mother and son like this: "Her noted son awaited her in the market-place, as she drove up in her little cart loaded with vegetables. Assisting her mother to alight the French president gave her his arm and escorted her to her accustomed seat. Then holding over her a large umbrella to shield her from the threatening weather he seated himself at her side and mother and son enjoyed a long talk together."

I have here at home an acquaintance who had a hard struggle to get a start in the world. When he became prosperous and built his beautiful home he finished a suite of rooms in it especially for his mother and furnished it with all the conveniences and comforts possible. Although his mother lives with her son's family she is made to feel that this part of the house is her own and that she has as much independence as she might desire. Every son or daughter should be ambitious to provide for their mother to the degree that they are able. Their own family life will be enriched thereby.

Often there are great discrepancies between the values, interests and need of various age groups but the confrontations among members of these groups does not need to be painful and destructive. Not only in home life but also in the outside world, both in the arena of enterprise and in the more broadly social sphere, you should pursue an acquaintance among all age-groups. In this age of increased anonymity and impersonality cling to the relationships you have cherished and foster them. Deepen the ties you have with family and friends.

Whomever else you neglect take no chances of giving your mother pain by neglecting her and thus making yourself miserable in the future. One of the most painful things I have ever witnessed was the anguish of a son who had become wealthy and in his prosperity neglected his mother whose sacrifices alone had made his success possible. He did not take the time to write to her more than once or twice a year. He was too busy to send a good long letter. Nor did he use the telephone to find out how she was doing back in his rural home town. Finally, when he was summoned to her bedside during her last illness and he realized that while he had been making his way in the city his mother had been for years without the ordinary comforts of life, he broke down completely. While he did everything possible to alleviate her suffering in the last few days that remained to her on earth and though he gave her an imposing burial, what torture he must have suffered at the sight of his neglected mother!

What a pathetic story of neglect many a mother's letters from her grown-up children could tell! A few lines, a sentence or two hurriedly written and mailed, often merely to ease a troubled conscience or worse yet, brief apologies for letters unwritten—these chill the mother's heart. The parental heart never changes in these respects and if anything it only grows more appreciative of the little attentions and thoughtful acts which meant so much to them in their younger days.

The maternal role as such is everywhere debunked today, whether flagrantly or subtly. It is viewed almost as a vice. Businesses use it as an excuse for sentimentalizing the exploitation of a dependence. Parenthood has been abused in this fashion and we all know instances of such exploitation. Yet the relation between mother and child still remains the most sacred natural tie that exists in human experience. All other loves are enriched by the nurturing spirit of the truly maternal.

One of the most pathetic triumphs of the sayings "Love is blind" is the story of the poor and aging mother whose life had been broken in the process of raising her children. She was visiting one of her sons in the penitentiary and he had been abandoned by everybody but herself. Poor old woman! It did not matter that he was a criminal— the mother's heart went out to him. To her this man was not some outcast from society but her darling boy and the child that God had given her.

The love of this woman might very well have been the sort of sublime feeling that is praised in all healthy cultures or it might have been a residual feeling of the sort that sociologists and psychologists delight in explaining. Surely a great potential for perfecting the world remains in the pure passion of maternal love. Those who have benefitted from a "Foster Mother" in their lives know the barrenness of life before they were taken under her wing.

No matter how callous or ungrateful a child may be, no matter how far he or she has strayed from his roots or her foundations, if there has been a true mother in his or her life then that mother will follow them to the grave if she is alive to get there. The knowledge of the existence of this maternal figure keeps many a grown child on the right path and gives many hope in their future. This unpractical love, this unselfish passion, has been sustenance and inspiration to people in all ages and places.

What gives us the idea that we have outgrown it?

Chapter 17

Religion

Everyone has a God of some sort and everyone worships at some altar in their heart. People expect tremendous things of their God. They expect their God and Creator to be liberal with an abundance of health and they ask God to shower material blessings upon them and to bestow all good things upon them without question. Yet they are contemptible in their own philanthropy, in their assistance of others, and in their donations to church or other charities.

Many people seem to think that the Creator is some power entirely separate from human beings and that their dealings must be directly with God. For this reason they do not feel the need to invest time or money in philanthropic institutions. We must realize that our attitude towards our fellow humans, towards the poor and the unfortunate, constitute our treatment of God and of God's children. Most people know the biblical quote: "In as much as ye have done it unto the least of these my brethren, ye have done it unto Me."

I knew a man who said that he thanked God that there was one good thing left in the world that was free—his religion. He did not believe that his religion cost him over a dollar a year. He obviously got more than a dollar's worth of his religion annually. Many complacent worshipers treat their religions as slot machines. If this is our mentality, then when we put a dollar in the collection basket we should expect to receive only a dollar's worth of sublimity.

We get out of a thing what we put into it. Commitment to God should permeate out entire lives and shape the way we treat our fellow creatures. If our devotion is limited to the proper donation in the collection basket (somewhat like a proper tip in a restaurant), we show that we regard our church as a kind of servicing of our psyches comparable to the servicing of the car at the corner garage. There is nothing wrong with enjoying the celebration of God as Creator and Friend socially. It is a great privilege to be able to do so and, indeed, proper in the most exact sense of the word. Yet we owe our God more than a bit of our time and portion of our money.

It is our acts that open or close the gates of our minds and hearts. Our acts cannot pour blessing upon us and crown our lives with the profoundest riches of human experience when we are miserly to our beliefs.

We limit our own capacity to receive with our lack of generosity in giving.

We know that we can only expect a narrow education if we are limited in our studies. We must give liberally before we receive in every department of life. I have never known a person who grudged his time, sympathy and money to ever get much out of philanthropy.

There truly is a road to God, the steps of which have been delineated many times in many different religions. All paths to God, however simple or complex, is characterized by development of an awareness of presence of God. It may seem very difficult to cultivate this awareness but it is possible to do so everyday, even in the busiest life. Awareness of the world in relation to the Divinity follows. The perspective this awareness provides enables us to examine ourselves in depth. We are not afraid to acknowledge our weaknesses, failings and wrong-doings when we rest in the assurance of the ability of God to forgive correct and transform.

Do not be afraid to expect the Creator to flood your life with good things and intangible blessings. What we receive, however, can come only through certain channels —which are opened only by our own generosity and confidence in God. If these are closed even God cannot reach us.

Sometimes it appears that we are clamoring for aid and are not heard; that we participate in an elaborate game and cannot lead honest lives; that we are in agony, and are not relieved of our pain. In some corner of our mind, in some moment of our day, we must learn to detach ourselves from whatever large horror or small irritations are grinding us down.

It is the large-hearted, generous person who makes it possible for God to give. If we are liberal and open-handed our harvest will be rich and abundant. Small souls cut off their own supply of emotional and spiritual sustenance by their narrow-ness and pettiness. There is a saying found in most religions concerning increasing our returns in life. The Bible, for exam-ple, states it like this: "Give and it shall be given unto thee."

Haven't you known people too contemptible to get very much out of life? It pains them to give up anything. They have not learned that there is an ocean of generosity out there upon which they can rest without ever tiring. Give yourself the most precious gift of all, a personal relationship with your God. Be generous with others systematically rather than at whim. Disci-pline yourself to withstand arid times.

If we remember how much we owe our God we can never make ourselves unhappy by the worst kind of wrongdoing. Like the maternal love which follows us to the grave from whatever source it has sprung, the love of God, once it has found us, will never leave us. We may forget it and we may lack the feeling that it is there but it will always carry us through the worst times. It will heighten all out joys. It will sow in our hearts unknown crops of future bliss.

God bless you and......

Be Good to Yourself

Orison Sewett Marden

Index

C

www.ingramcontent.com/pod-product-compliance
Lightning Source LLC
Chambersburg PA
CBHW071002040426
42443CB00007B/619